OPPOSING VIEWPOINTS® SERIES

| Pesticides and GMOs

Other Books of Related Interest

Opposing Viewpoints Series

Corporate Farming
The Environment
Genetic Engineering
Global Sustainability
The Politics of Water Scarcity

At Issue Series

Adaptation and Climate Change
Environmental Racism and Classism
Food Insecurity
Food Safety
Genetically Modified Food

Current Controversies Series

Biodiversity
Conserving the Environment
Genetic Engineering
The Global Food Crisis
Vegetarianism

> "Congress shall make no law ... abridging the freedom of speech, or of the press."

First Amendment to the US Constitution

The basic foundation of our democracy is the First Amendment guarantee of freedom of expression. The Opposing Viewpoints series is dedicated to the concept of this basic freedom and the idea that it is more important to practice it than to enshrine it.

OPPOSING
VIEWPOINTS®
SERIES

| Pesticides and GMOs

Yea Jee Bae, Book Editor

GREENHAVEN
PUBLISHING

Published in 2019 by Greenhaven Publishing, LLC
353 3rd Avenue, Suite 255, New York, NY 10010

Articles in Greenhaven Publishing anthologies are often edited for length to meet page
requirements. In addition, original titles of these works are changed to clearly present
the main thesis and to explicitly indicate the author's opinion. Every effort is made to
ensure that Greenhaven Publishing accurately reflects the original intent of the authors.
Every effort has been made to trace the owners of the copyrighted material.

Cover image: Adriano Kirihara/Shutterstock.com

Library of Congress Cataloging-in-Publication Data

Names: Bae, Yea Jee, editor.
Title: Pesticides and GMOs / Yea Jee Bae, book editor.
Other titles: Pesticides and genetically modified organisms | Opposing
  viewpoints series (Unnumbered).
Description: First edition. | New York : Greenhaven Publishing, 2019. |
  Series: Opposing viewpoints | Includes bibliographical references and
  index. | Audience: Grades 9–12.
Identifiers: LCCN 2018029331| ISBN 9781534504141 (library bound) | ISBN
  9781534504394 (pbk.)
Subjects: LCSH: Pesticides. | Transgenic organisms.
Classification: LCC SB951 .P4418 2019 | DDC 628.5/29—dc23
LC record available at https://lccn.loc.gov/2018029331

Manufactured in the United States of America

Website: http://greenhavenpublishing.com

Contents

Chapter 1: Do the Benefits of Pesticides Outweigh Their Dangers?

Chapter 2: How Do Pesticides and GMOs Affect the Agriculture Industry?

The Importance of Opposing Viewpoints

Perhaps every generation experiences a period in time in which the populace seems especially polarized, starkly divided on the important issues of the day and gravitating toward the far ends of the political spectrum and away from a consensus-facilitating middle ground. The world that today's students are growing up in and that they will soon enter into as active and engaged citizens is deeply fragmented in just this way. Issues relating to terrorism, immigration, women's rights, minority rights, race relations, health care, taxation, wealth and poverty, the environment, policing, military intervention, the proper role of government—in some ways, perennial issues that are freshly and uniquely urgent and vital with each new generation—are currently roiling the world.

If we are to foster a knowledgeable, responsible, active, and engaged citizenry among today's youth, we must provide them with the intellectual, interpretive, and critical-thinking tools and experience necessary to make sense of the world around them and of the all-important debates and arguments that inform it. After all, the outcome of these debates will in large measure determine the future course, prospects, and outcomes of the world and its peoples, particularly its youth. If they are to become successful members of society and productive and informed citizens, students need to learn how to evaluate the strengths and weaknesses of someone else's arguments, how to sift fact from opinion and fallacy, and how to test the relative merits and validity of their own opinions against the known facts and the best possible available information. The landmark series Opposing Viewpoints has been providing students with just such critical-thinking skills and exposure to the debates surrounding society's most urgent contemporary issues for many years, and it continues to serve this essential role with undiminished commitment, care, and rigor.

The key to the series's success in achieving its goal of sharpening students' critical-thinking and analytic skills resides in its title—

Opposing Viewpoints. In every intriguing, compelling, and engaging volume of this series, readers are presented with the widest possible spectrum of distinct viewpoints, expert opinions, and informed argumentation and commentary, supplied by some of today's leading academics, thinkers, analysts, politicians, policy makers, economists, activists, change agents, and advocates. Every opinion and argument anthologized here is presented objectively and accorded respect. There is no editorializing in any introductory text or in the arrangement and order of the pieces. No piece is included as a "straw man," an easy ideological target for cheap point-scoring. As wide and inclusive a range of viewpoints as possible is offered, with no privileging of one particular political ideology or cultural perspective over another. It is left to each individual reader to evaluate the relative merits of each argument—as he or she sees it, and with the use of ever-growing critical-thinking skills—and grapple with his or her own assumptions, beliefs, and perspectives to determine how convincing or successful any given argument is and how the reader's own stance on the issue may be modified or altered in response to it.

This process is facilitated and supported by volume, chapter, and selection introductions that provide readers with the essential context they need to begin engaging with the spotlighted issues, with the debates surrounding them, and with their own perhaps shifting or nascent opinions on them. In addition, guided reading and discussion questions encourage readers to determine the authors' point of view and purpose, interrogate and analyze the various arguments and their rhetoric and structure, evaluate the arguments' strengths and weaknesses, test their claims against available facts and evidence, judge the validity of the reasoning, and bring into clearer, sharper focus the reader's own beliefs and conclusions and how they may differ from or align with those in the collection or those of their classmates.

Research has shown that reading comprehension skills improve dramatically when students are provided with compelling, intriguing, and relevant "discussable" texts. The subject matter of these collections could not be more compelling, intriguing, or urgently relevant to today's students and the world they are poised to inherit. The anthologized articles and the reading and discussion questions that are included with them also provide the basis for stimulating, lively, and passionate classroom debates. Students who are compelled to anticipate objections to their own argument and identify the flaws in those of an opponent read more carefully, think more critically, and steep themselves in relevant context, facts, and information more thoroughly. In short, using discussable text of the kind provided by every single volume in the Opposing Viewpoints series encourages close reading, facilitates reading comprehension, fosters research, strengthens critical thinking, and greatly enlivens and energizes classroom discussion and participation. The entire learning process is deepened, extended, and strengthened.

For all of these reasons, Opposing Viewpoints continues to be exactly the right resource at exactly the right time—when we most need to provide readers with the critical-thinking tools and skills that will not only serve them well in school but also in their careers and their daily lives as decision-making family members, community members, and citizens. This series encourages respectful engagement with and analysis of opposing viewpoints and fosters a resulting increase in the strength and rigor of one's own opinions and stances. As such, it helps make readers "future ready," and that readiness will pay rich dividends for the readers themselves, for the citizenry, for our society, and for the world at large.

Introduction

> "To make the changes we need to make and to reach a safer future, we will need the resources of everybody here—the scientists, the policy makers, and the industrialists—all working together towards a common goal. And that goal is a planet that can continue to support life."
>
> —Dr. Piers Sellers (1955–2016), Acting Director of NASA's Earth Science Division

As the world's population continues to grow exponentially, increasing crop yields to feed the inhabitants of our planet becomes ever the more challenging, but it is a problem that must be solved. Under our current model of farming, prevalent pesticide usage and genetically modified crops are the route that large industry farms have decided to take as the solution to growing the amount of food necessary for the global market. However, new scientific analysis now suggests that agroecology methods—farming techniques that apply ecological processes to agriculture—may be more sustainable and effective in the long-term. To effectively evaluate these differing approaches, a nuanced understanding of pesticides and GMOs is essential.

Since the years following World War II, chemical pesticides have experienced a boom to become a widespread and integrated part of modern agricultural production. On a worldwide scale, pesticide use has increased in most regions and created a global market worth billions of dollars. However, as pesticide usage climbs, environmental and health risks as a direct result of their prolific and excessive use rises as well. People around the world are exposed to low levels of pesticide residues in their food even if they don't live near farming communities, and environmental degradation has become a serious concern. Concurrently, the indirect detrimental effects of pesticides can be seen in societal and economic spheres as well. While pesticides undoubtedly do work for pest control and the protection of crops, the degree of their effectiveness has been called into question, and perhaps more importantly, we are now inquiring whether or not the tradeoff of their ill effects is worth the gains.

GMOs are a controversial subject as well, as they have been since their introduction to the public. Today, genetically modified crops make up a great deal of the world's crops with some specific varieties outnumbering the amount of non-GM crops of the same type. In the United States, for instance, as of 2017, over 90 percent of our soybeans and corn are grown from genetically modified seeds. Indeed, for the past 20 years, much of the food we've been consuming has been genetically modified. Yet despite how commonplace GMOs have become in our everyday lives, the public opinion on them is not one of acceptance but fear and rejection. Anxious about potential health risks that may be discovered down the line, consumers are often afraid to knowingly eat GM foods and push for more regulatory measures on them. In the scientific community, the attitude appears to be flipped with the majority asserting the safety of GMOs, but even here, dissension exists and is expressed in ongoing debates. To find answers, keeping these lines of communication open is vital.

The questions and concerns surrounding these topics are multi-layered and complex, requiring careful review and analysis of myriad viewpoints to gain a well-balanced understanding of the debated issues. *Opposing Viewpoints: Pesticides and GMOs* works to introduce readers to this academic investigation by examining pesticide use and the GMO controversy in chapters titled "Do the Benefits of Pesticides Outweigh Their Dangers?," "How Do

Pesticides and GMOs Affect the Agriculture Industry?," "Do GMOs Pose a Threat to Our Health?," and "Do Pesticides and GMOs Need Stricter Regulation?" With thoughtful processing of the varied perspectives offered by numerous scientists, journalists, industry experts, and more, readers can begin forming their own answers to the important challenges facing our world at this crucial juncture.

OPPOSING
VIEWPOINTS®
SERIES

CHAPTER 1

Do the Benefits of Pesticides Outweigh Their Dangers?

Chapter Preface

M odern pesticides are chemicals utilized for killing or repelling organisms that negatively impact food production or human health. They are designed to be toxic to a target group of organisms, but they can often have negative effects that spill over into non-targets like humans and the environment. Coming in different varieties for specific needs, such as herbicides, insecticides, fungicides, and more, pesticides help farmers to stay afloat in a highly competitive market by increasing profits and lowering risks. Also called crop-protection products by those in agriculture, proponents of pesticides point to them as having improved the sustainability of food production. The United States alone makes up more than 25 percent of the global pesticides market.

Used to protect crops from insects, diseases, and weeds, pesticides allow for greater yields due to less crop loss. Additionally, these chemicals have been effective measures for stopping the spread of disease-carrying pests, protecting humans from sickness like West Nile Virus, malaria, and yellow fever. However, these benefits do not come without a price tag to pay.

As aforementioned, pesticides can have hazardous effects, especially when used excessively or without following proper practices. In developing countries where small farmers often use pesticides without appropriate education and training, pesticide poisoning is a serious problem that must be addressed. Workers who interact directly with the chemicals are at high risk, as are the communities surrounding farms where pesticide drift can occur. Many pesticides end up in areas and on targets they were not intended for, leading to the contamination of the environment and upsetting the natural balance of ecosystems. Pesticide residue has also been found in food, and these health and environmental issues can result in mild to fatal effects for both humans and wildlife.

The following chapter examines the dangers and benefits of pesticides, as well as issues pertaining to their use.

> *"From field to fork the use of pesticides ensures that people and the environment are exposed to potentially harmful risks from these toxic chemicals that are designed to kill."*

Pesticides Should Only Be a Last Resort

Nick Mole

In the following viewpoint, Nick Mole argues that pesticides should only be used as a last resort when all other crop protection methods have failed. He states that using pesticides prolifically doesn't necessarily protect crops better, but it does increase exposure risks and contamination, leading to severely toxic effects on workers, consumers, and the environment. Mole is a policy officer and program coordinator in the Pesticide Action Network UK. He studied environmental science in university and worked six years as a campaigner for the Environmental Investigation Agency.

As you read, consider the following questions:

1. According to Mole, what are the factors that pressure farmers to use increasing amounts of pesticides?
2. According to the viewpoint, what percentage of the food purchased in the UK has pesticide residues on it?
3. According to Mole, what are easily achievable methods for reducing pesticide use?

"Consumers and Farm Workers at Risk from Toxic Pesticides Sprayed on Salad," by Nick Mole, The Resurgence Trust, September 1, 2011. Reprinted by permission.

Pesticides of one sort or another are used to produce 95 per cent of the produce grown in the UK and are promoted by the companies that make them as being the only way to ensure that yields remain high, prices remain low, and that growers can make a living. However, this is far from the truth, and many studies show that it is possible to maintain yields and profitability with reduced pesticide inputs by working with nature rather than against it.

The problem is that reliance on agrochemicals, and pesticides in particular, is hardwired into our current agricultural system. Factors such as the demands of supermarkets for perfect produce, the limited range of varieties available to farmers, monocrop systems and crop rotations that create ideal conditions for pests to develop all place pressure on farmers to use more and more pesticides with devastating consequences for the environment and human health.

From field to fork the use of pesticides ensures that people and the environment are exposed to potentially harmful risks from these toxic chemicals that are designed to kill. In the UK over 20,000 tonnes of pesticides are sprayed on farmland annually to grow the food that we eat.

Toxic Threats

A great number of these chemicals are potentially toxic to humans, pollute waterways and have harmful effects on our biodiversity as has been seen by the recent loss of bees and other pollinators here in the UK and elsewhere.

We know that the impacts of pesticides are incredibly serious. In 2008, a European parliament commissioned study concluded that the families of farm workers are far more susceptible to childhood leukaemia's than the general population. It is also estimated that 25 million agricultural workers suffer at least one incident of pesticide poisoning annually. And you can add to this all the unreported poisonings of bystanders and residents that occur throughout the pesticide spraying season.

All along the production trail people—whether it is the grower, the picker, the packager, local residents and bystanders or the end consumer—are exposed to pesticides.

Pesticides are used from the very earliest stage of production—and can be applied to the very seeds themselves. Dressing seeds with pesticides prior to planting is touted as a "safe" way of applying pesticides that will reduce human exposure. Under this approach, the insecticides are taken up into the structure of the plant as it grows making the plant itself poisonous to its pests. What this also means is that the pesticide remains in the plant even after harvesting and no amount of washing or cooking will eradicate it.

But farmers and farmworkers are also exposed through handling the seeds. Many do not realise that the seeds are toxic and they—and neighbouring residents—can be contaminated by the pesticides covered dust that is kicked up and dispersed.

Exposure Risks

Other fungicides, herbicides and insecticides are applied throughout the growth cycle of the plant to opening up yet further potential routes of exposure. The pesticide applicator, while at greatest risk, is usually required to wear protective equipment to reduce exposure. But others are not so lucky.

One particular group, that has been neglected by successive UK governments, is rural residents. People who live in the countryside can be exposed to pesticides during and after spraying in fields close to their homes. This exposure can go on for years and increases the risk of chronic illnesses including some cancers and neurological diseases like Parkinson's.

Workers in the fields are also open to exposure as they walk amongst the crops and particularly if they are put in the fields soon after the crops are sprayed.

In particular, labourers employed to harvest the crops can be exposed to pesticides that remain on the crops whilst they pick them. Even after leaving the field, exposure is still possible on clothes that have been contaminated with pesticides taken home for washing or often used again the next day.

The problems can be exacerbated by the fact that many of the labourers used to harvest and pack produce in the UK do not have English as their first language and so cannot understand warnings about what they need to do to minimise or avoid the risk of pesticide contamination. Their status also often limits their ability to report any incidents of pesticide poisoning that might occur and so these incidents go largely unreported in the UK.

And finally, the end consumer will come into contact with pesticides as residues on the food that they eat. The DEFRA Expert Committee on Pesticide Residues in Food (PRiF) samples a range of produce each year. This sampling shows that 30-40 per cent of the food purchased in the UK has pesticide residues present on it—and often multiple residues are present.

Chemical Warfare

Multiple pesticide residues are particularly concerning because some pesticides can interact with one another and increase their toxicity—the so-called cocktail effect. If we take lettuce as an example there are 122 registered professional pesticides that can be used for growing lettuces in the UK of those:

- 20 are fungicides
- 45 are herbicides
- 57 are insecticides

Amongst them are some particularly unpleasant actives:

Mancozeb, a fungicide that is also classified as a carcinogen, a developmental or reproductive toxin, a suspected endocrine disruptor and a potential groundwater contaminant. Pirimicarb, an insecticide and also classified as a carcinogen and a cholinesterase inhibitor. Lambda-cyhalothrin, an insecticide and suspected endocrine disruptor. Cypermethrin, an insecticide and classified as a possible carcinogen and suspected endocrine disruptor.

Fungicides are applied to the soil even before sowing. If the lettuce is grown under cover, it is possible that two to three applications of fungicides could be used as well as an insecticide.

The Pesticide Action Network UK has analysed the figures made available by PRiF between the years 2000 and 2006 and found that of 826 non-organic lettuces tested, 36.7 per cent contained pesticide residues with 19.5 per cent containing a cocktail of residues.

Because lettuces along with many other crops such as soft fruits are considered to be high value crops, farmers will often use pesticides prophylactically in a bid to head off pest damage rather than to treat an existing pest problem. Unnecessary applications result in higher usage and on the whole don't ensure that the crop will actually be any better protected.

Significant reductions in pesticide use are easily achievable simply by changing crop rotations, or using resistant varieties can dramatically. But this requires a fundamental shift in the approach away from pesticides first to pesticides last. This means that pesticides would only be used when all other methods have failed and then they would be used in a targeted manner ensuring that what is used is the least toxic option available. It requires working with, rather than against, nature and if we do so, we will all benefit.

"For developing countries it is imperative to use pesticides, as no one would prefer famine and communicable diseases like malaria. It may thus be expedient to accept a reasonable degree of risk."

Pesticide Use Can Be Justified

Wasim Aktar, Dwaipayan Sengupta, and Ashim Chowdhury

In the following viewpoint, excerpted for length, Wasim Aktar, Dwaipayan Sengupta, and Ashim Chowdhury argue that despite the undeniable contamination to the environment and adverse health effects, pesticide use can be justified. Rather than making a generalized decision on whether pesticides are good or bad, the authors propose that pesticide usage should be considered on a risk-benefit model specific to the case in question. Aktar is a research scientist and former research fellow at the Department of Agricultural Chemicals at Bidhan Chandra Agricultural University. Sengupta and Chowdhury are affiliated with the Department of Agricultural Chemistry and Soil Science at the University of Calcutta.

Aktar, W., Sengupta, D., and Chowdhury, A. (2009). Impact of Pesticides Use in Agriculture: Their Benefits and Hazards. *Interdisciplinary Toxicology,* 2(1), Slovak Toxicology Society SETOX, 2009, pp. 1-12. Reprinted by permission.

As you read, consider the following questions:

1. According to the viewpoint, how are secondary benefits of pesticide use different from primary benefits?
2. According to the viewpoint, how is the total cost-benefit of pesticide use different between developed and developing countries?
3. According to the viewpoint, what is the reason for the imbalance in the amount of published literature for and against pesticides?

The term pesticide covers a wide range of compounds including insecticides, fungicides, herbicides, rodenticides, molluscicides, nematicides, plant growth regulators and others. Among these, organochlorine (OC) insecticides, used successfully in controlling a number of diseases, such as malaria and typhus, were banned or restricted after the 1960s in most of the technologically advanced countries. The introduction of other synthetic insecticides—organophosphate (OP) insecticides in the 1960s, carbamates in 1970s and pyrethroids in 1980s and the introduction of herbicides and fungicides in the 1970s–1980s contributed greatly to pest control and agricultural output. Ideally a pesticide must be lethal to the targeted pests, but not to non-target species, including man. Unfortunately, this is not the case, so the controversy of use and abuse of pesticides has surfaced. The rampant use of these chemicals, under the adage, "if little is good, a lot more will be better" has played havoc with human and other life forms.

[…]

Benefits of Pesticides

The primary benefits are the consequences of the pesticides' effects—the direct gains expected from their use. For example the effect of killing caterpillars feeding on the crop brings the primary benefit of higher yields and better quality of cabbage. The three main effects result in 26 primary benefits ranging from protection of recreational turf to saved human lives. The secondary benefits are the less immediate or less obvious benefits that result from the primary benefits. They may be subtle, less intuitively obvious, or of longer term. It follows that for secondary benefits it is therefore more difficult to establish cause and effect, but nevertheless they can be powerful justifications for pesticide use. For example the higher cabbage yield might bring additional revenue that could be put towards children's education or medical care, leading to a healthier, better educated population. There are various secondary benefits identified, ranging from fitter people to conserved biodiversity.

Improving Productivity

Tremendous benefits have been derived from the use of pesticides in forestry, public health and the domestic sphere—and, of course, in agriculture, a sector upon which the Indian economy is largely dependent. Food grain production, which stood at a mere 50 million tons in 1948–49, had increased almost fourfold to 198 million tons by the end of 1996–97 from an estimated 169 million hectares of permanently cropped land. This result has been achieved by the use of high-yield varieties of seeds, advanced irrigation technologies and agricultural chemicals (Employment Information: Indian Labour Statistics, 1994). Similarly outputs and productivity have increased dramatically in most countries, for example wheat yields in the United Kingdom, corn yields in the USA. Increases in productivity have been due to several factors including use of fertiliser, better varieties and use of machinery. Pesticides have been an integral part of the process by reducing losses from the weeds, diseases and insect pests that can markedly reduce the amount of harvestable produce. Warren (1998) also drew attention to the spectacular increases in crop yields in the United States in the twentieth century. Webster et al. (1999) stated that "considerable economic losses" would be suffered without pesticide use and quantified the significant increases in yield and economic margin that result from pesticide use. Moreover, in the environment most pesticides undergo photochemical transformation to produce metabolites which are relatively non-toxic to both human beings and the environment (Kole et al., 1999).

Protection of Crop Losses/Yield Reduction

In medium land, rice even under puddle conditions during the critical period warranted an effective and economic weed control practice to prevent reduction in rice yield due to weeds that ranged from 28 to 48%, based on comparisons that included control (weedy) plots (Behera and Singh, 1999). Weeds reduce yield of dry land crops (Behera and Singh, 1999) by 37–79%. Severe infestation of weeds, particularly in the early stage of crop establishment, ultimately accounts for a yield reduction of 40%. Herbicides provided both an economic and labour benefit.

Vector Disease Control

Vector-borne diseases are most effectively tackled by killing the vectors. Insecticides are often the only practical way to control the insects that spread deadly diseases such as malaria, resulting in an estimated 5000 deaths each day (Ross, 2005). In 2004, Bhatia wrote that malaria is one of the leading causes of morbidity and mortality in the developing world and a major public health problem in India. Disease control strategies are crucially important also for livestock.

Quality of Food

In countries of the first world, it has been observed that a diet containing fresh fruit and vegetables far outweigh potential risks from eating very low residues of pesticides in crops (Brown, 2004). Increasing evidence (Dietary Guidelines, 2005) shows that eating fruit and vegetables regularly reduces the risk of many cancers, high blood pressure, heart disease, diabetes, stroke, and other chronic diseases.

Lewis et al. (2005) discussed the nutritional properties of apples and blueberries in the US diet and concluded that their high concentrations of antioxidants act as protectants against cancer and heart disease. Lewis attributed doubling in wild blueberry production and subsequent increases in consumption chiefly to herbicide use that improved weed control.

Other Areas—Transport, Sport Complex, Building

The transport sector makes extensive use of pesticides, particularly herbicides. Herbicides and insecticides are used to maintain the turf on sports pitches, cricket grounds and golf courses. Insecticides protect buildings and other wooden structures from damage by termites and woodboring insects.

Hazards of Pesticides

Direct Impact on Humans

If the credits of pesticides include enhanced economic potential in terms of increased production of food and fibre, and amelioration of vector-borne diseases, then their debits have resulted in serious health implications to man and his environment. There is now overwhelming evidence that some of these chemicals do pose a potential risk to humans and other life forms and unwanted side effects to the environment (Forget, 1993; Igbedioh, 1991; Jeyaratnam, 1981). No segment of the population is completely protected against exposure to pesticides and the potentially serious health effects, though a disproportionate burden, is shouldered by the people of developing countries and by high risk groups in each country (WHO, 1990). The world-wide deaths and chronic diseases due to pesticide poisoning number about 1 million per year (Environews Forum, 1999).

The high risk groups exposed to pesticides include production workers, formulators, sprayers, mixers, loaders and agricultural farm workers. During manufacture and formulation, the possibility of hazards may be higher because the processes involved are not risk free. In industrial settings, workers are at increased risk since they handle various toxic chemicals including pesticides, raw materials, toxic solvents and inert carriers.

OC compounds could pollute the tissues of virtually every life form on the earth, the air, the lakes and the oceans, the fishes that live in them and the birds that feed on the fishes (Hurley et al., 1998). The US National Academy of Sciences stated that the DDT metabolite DDE causes eggshell thinning and that the bald eagle population in the United States declined primarily because of exposure to DDT and its metabolites (Liroff, 2000). Certain environmental chemicals, including pesticides termed as endocrine disruptors, are known to elicit their adverse effects by mimicking or antagonising natural hormones in the body and it has been postulated that their long-term, low-dose exposure is increasingly linked to human health effects such as immune suppression, hormone disruption, diminished intelligence, reproductive abnormalities and cancer (Brouwer et al., 1999; Crisp et al., 1998; Hurley et al., 1998)

[...]

Impact on Environment

Pesticides can contaminate soil, water, turf, and other vegetation. In addition to killing insects or weeds, pesticides can be toxic to a host of other organisms including birds, fish, beneficial insects, and non-target plants. Insecticides are generally the most acutely toxic class of pesticides, but herbicides can also pose risks to non-target organisms.

Surface Water Contamination

Pesticides can reach surface water through runoff from treated plants and soil. Contamination of water by pesticides is widespread. The results of a comprehensive set of studies done by the US Geological Survey (USGS) on major river basins across the country in the early to mid- 90s yielded startling results. More than 90 percent of water and fish samples from all streams contained one, or more often, several pesticides (Kole et al; 2001). Pesticides were found in all samples from major rivers with mixed agricultural and urban land use influences and 99 percent of samples of urban streams (Bortleson and Davis, 1987–1995). The USGS also found that concentrations of insecticides in urban streams commonly exceeded guidelines for protection of aquatic life (US Geological

Survey, 1999). Twenty-three pesticides were detected in waterways in the Puget Sound Basin, including 17 herbicides. According to USGS, more pesticides were detected in urban streams than in agricultural streams (US Department of the Interior, 1995). The herbicides 2,4-D, diuron, and prometon, and the insecticides chlorpyrifos and diazinon, all commonly used by urban homeowners and school districts, were among the 21 pesticides detected most often in surface and ground water across the nation (US Geological Survey, 1998). Trifluralin and 2,4-D were found in water samples collected in 19 out of the 20 river basins studied (Bevans et al., 1998; Fenelon et al., 1998; Levings et al., 1998; Wall et al., 1998). The USGS also found that concentrations of insecticides in urban streams commonly exceeded guidelines for protection of aquatic life (US Geological Survey, 1999). According to USGS, "in general more pesticides were detected in urban streams than in agricultural streams" (Bortleson and Davis, 1987–1995). The herbicide 2,4-D was the most commonly found pesticide, detected in 12 out of 13 streams. The insecticide diazinon, and the weed-killers dichlobenil, diuron, triclopyr, and glyphosate were detected also in Puget Sound basin streams. Both diazinon and diuron were found at levels exceeding concentrations recommended by the National Academy of Sciences for the protection of aquatic life (Bortleson and Davis, 1987–1995).

Ground Water Contamination
Groundwater pollution due to pesticides is a worldwide problem. According to the USGS, at least 143 different pesticides and 21 transformation products have been found in ground water, including pesticides from every major chemical class. Over the past two decades, detections have been found in the ground water of more than 43 states (Waskom, 1994). During one survey in India, 58% of drinking water samples drawn from various hand pumps and wells around Bhopal were contaminated with organochlorine pesticides above the EPA standards (Kole and Bagchi, 1995). Once ground water is polluted with toxic chemicals, it may take many

years for the contamination to dissipate or be cleaned up. Cleanup may also be very costly and complex, if not impossible (Waskom 1994; O'Neil, 1998; US EPA, 2001).

Soil Contamination

A large number of transformation products (TPs) from a wide range of pesticides have been documented (Barcelo' and Hennion, 1997; Roberts, 1998; Roberts and Hutson, 1999). Not many of all possible pesticide TPs have been monitored in soil, showing that there is a pressing need for more studies in this field. Persistency and movement of these pesticides and their TPs are determined by some parameters, such as water solubility, soil-sorption constant (Koc), the octanol/water partition coefficient (Kow), and half-life in soil (DT50). Pesticides and TPs could be grouped into: (a) Hydrophobic, persistent, and bioaccumulable pesticides that are strongly bound to soil. Pesticides that exhibit such behavior include the organochlorine DDT, endosulfan, endrin, heptachlor, lindane and their TPs. Most of them are now banned in agriculture but their residues are still present. (b) Polar pesticides are represented mainly by herbicides but they include also carbamates, fungicides and some organophosphorus insecticide TPs. They can be moved from soil by runoff and leaching, thereby constituting a problem for the supply of drinking water to the population. The most researched pesticide TPs in soil are undoubtedly those from herbicides. Several metabolic pathways have been suggested, involving transformation through hydrolysis, methylation, and ring cleavage that produce several toxic phenolic compounds. The pesticides and their TPs are retained by soils to different degrees, depending on the interactions between soil and pesticide properties. The most influential soil characteristic is the organic matter content. The larger the organic matter content, the greater the adsorption of pesticides and TPs. The capacity of the soil to hold positively charged ions in an exchangeable form is important with paraquat and other pesticides that are positively charged. Strong mineral acid is required for extracting these chemicals,

PESTICIDES ARE HELPING INDIA

India's farmers are hard at work. Not only do they help to feed a nation that contains 1.3 billion people—one fifth of the world's population—but they also produce around 20 percent of the world's cotton. However their productivity is threatened by pests that can ruin their crops and their livelihoods. Here's a glimpse of how plant science is helping reduce the threat.

According to a study by the Associated Chambers of Commerce and Industry of India, annual crop losses due to pests and diseases amount to Rs.50,000 crore ($500 billion), which is significant in a country where at least 200 million Indians go to bed hungry every night. The value of plant science is therefore huge.

Take pulse crops: Indians rely heavily on chick peas, pigeon peas, mung beans and lentils for their daily protein requirements, and these are an essential ingredient in many native dishes, but it is estimated that without crop protection products the pulse crop yield can fall by around 30%.

Given the benefits of crop protection are so significant, small-scale farmers across India are trained in the responsible use of crop protection products. For example in the Adoni region of India a public-private partnership has trained more than 100,000 farmers to manage the threat of pests more effectively.

India is also well known for its cotton production, and it is the second biggest cotton producer in the world. Plant science plays a vital role at keeping insects at bay to keep cotton production and quality high. In 2002, India's farmers planted their first biotech crop, an insect-resistant cotton variety, which protects the plants from the specific insects which can destroy cotton crops.

Today Bt cotton accounts for more than 90 percent of cotton grown in Indian and the impact has been impressive—according to the study Economic Impacts and Impact Dynamics of Bt Cotton in India, Bt cotton has helped India's smallholder farmers increase yield by 24 percent and raise their incomes by 50 percent.

Plant science is keeping India's insects in line.

"India's Farmers Fighting Pests," CropLife International, May 5, 2015.

without any analytical improvement or study reported in recent years. Soil pH is also of some importance. Adsorption increases with decreasing soil pH for ionizable pesticides (e.g. 2,4-D,2,4,5-T, picloram, and atrazine) (Andreu and Pico', 2004).

[...]

Conclusion

The data on environmental-cum-health risk assessment studies may be regarded as an aid towards a better understanding of the problem. Data on the occurrence of pesticide-related illnesses among defined populations in developing countries are scanty. Generation of base-line descriptive epidemiological data based on area profiles, development of intervention strategies designed to lower the incidence of acute poisoning and periodic surveillance studies on high risk groups are needed. Our efforts should include investigations of outbreaks and accidental exposure to pesticides, correlation studies, cohort analyses, prospective studies and randomised trials of intervention procedures. Valuable information can be collected by monitoring the end product of human exposure in the form of residue levels in body fluids and tissues of the general population. The importance of education and training of workers as a major vehicle to ensure a safe use of pesticides is being increasingly recognised.

Because of the extensive benefits which man accrues from pesticides, these chemicals provide the best opportunity to those who juggle with the risk-benefit equations. The economic impact of pesticides in non-target species (including humans) has been estimated at approximately $8 billion annually in developing countries. What is required is to weigh all the risks against the benefits to ensure a maximum margin of safety. The total cost-benefit picture from pesticide use differs appreciably between developed and developing countries. For developing countries it is imperative to use pesticides, as no one would prefer famine and communicable diseases like malaria. It may thus be expedient to accept a reasonable degree of risk. Our approach to the use of pesticides should be pragmatic. In other words, all activities concerning pesticides should be based on scientific judgment and not on commercial considerations. There are some inherent difficulties in fully evaluating the risks to human health due to pesticides. For example there is a large number of human variables such as age, sex, race, socio-economic status, diet, state of health, etc.—all of which affect human exposure to pesticides. But practically little is known about the effects of these variables. The long-term effects of low level exposure to one pesticide are greatly influenced by concomitant exposure to other pesticides as well as to pollutants present in air, water, food and drugs.

Pesticides are often considered a quick, easy, and inexpensive solution for controlling weeds and insect pests in urban landscapes. However, pesticide use comes at a significant cost. Pesticides have contaminated almost every part of our environment. Pesticide residues are found in soil and air, and in surface and ground water across the countries, and urban pesticide uses contribute to the problem. Pesticide contamination poses significant risks to the environment and non-target organisms ranging from beneficial soil microorganisms, to insects, plants, fish, and birds. Contrary to common misconceptions, even herbicides can cause harm to the environment. In fact, weed killers can be especially problematic because they are used in relatively large volumes. The best way to reduce pesticide contamination (and the harm it causes) in our environment is for all of us to do our part to use safer, non-chemical pest control (including weed control) methods.

The exercise of analysing the range and nature of benefits arising from pesticide use has been a mixture of delving, dreaming and distillation. There have been blind alleys, but also positive surprises. The general picture is as we suspected: there is publicity, ideological kudos and scientific opportunity associated with "knocking" pesticides, while praising them brings accusations of vested interests. This is reflected in the imbalance in the number of published scientific papers, reports, newspaper articles and websites against and for pesticides. The colour coding for types of benefit, economic, social or environmental, reveals the fact that at community level, most of the benefits are social, with some compelling economic benefits. At national level, the benefits are principally economic, with some social benefits and one or two issues of environmental benefits. It is only at global level that the environmental benefits really come into play.

There is a need to convey the message that prevention of adverse health effects and promotion of health are profitable investments for employers and employees as a support to a sustainable development of economics. To sum up, based on our limited knowledge of direct and/or inferential information, the domain of pesticides illustrates a certain ambiguity in situations in which people are undergoing life-long exposure. There is thus every reason to develop health education packages based on knowledge, aptitude and practices and to disseminate them within the community in order to minimise human exposure to pesticides.

"*Those at greatest risk are those who experience the greatest exposures— typically smaller-holder farmers, farm workers and their families.*"

Pesticides Risk Human Health in Developing Countries

Forum for Agricultural Risk Management in Development

In the following viewpoint, excerpted for length, authors from the Forum for Agricultural Risk Management in Development argue that pesticide use is especially problematic and dangerous in developing countries due to excessive use and unsafe practices. The viewpoint claims that much of the pesticide available to these countries are of an inferior quality, and the population who uses them often do not have proper training and do not adhere to regulations. The Forum for Agricultural Risk Management in Development (FARMD) is a network of practitioners that seeks to share knowledge about agricultural risk management and strengthen investments in the agricultural sector.

"Integrated Pest Management," Agricultural Risk Management in Development, January 2005. Reprinted by permission.

As you read, consider the following questions:

1. According to the viewpoint, what are some externalities of pesticide use?
2. According to the viewpoint, for what reasons are smallholder farmers less likely to follow appropriate procedures for pesticide use?
3. According to the viewpoint, what factors contribute to the increasing pesticide-related health and environmental issues in developing countries?

[…]

Synthetic pesticides are potent nerve toxins to all living organisms, including humans. Many pesticides, especially those available and used very heavily in the developing world, are not specific to the pest on which they are used, and are highly toxic to a broad array of living things.

Humans can have both acute and chronic exposures to pesticides. Acute exposure includes large doses of pesticide that are inhaled, ingested, or absorbed through the skin. Chronic exposure consists of smaller amounts taken into the body with cumulative effects on health over time.

Those at greatest risk are those who experience the greatest exposures—typically smaller-holder farmers, farm workers and their families. These populations are also often the poorest members of society. Larger-holders are more likely to have received training on pesticide risk avoidance; however, laborers hired by them may not. Acute and chronic effects vary from pesticide to pesticide in both type and degree, and are listed below.

Acute Human Pesticide Exposure

Acute effects from some pesticides include death, vomiting, severe headache, skin damage, temporary blindness, shortness of breath, and uncontrollable nervous tremors.

Chronic Human Pesticide Exposure

Chronic exposure can result in cancers, mutations in unborn children, suppression of the immune system, reduced fertility and/or permanent damage to eyes, lungs, liver and other essential organs.

Environmental Impacts of Pesticide Use

Uncontrolled pesticide use can lead to several unintended and harmful environmental effects. These include contamination of soil and water, pesticide drift, effects on non-target organisms, disruption of natural pest controls leading to pest resurgence, and resistance. Economists have developed methods for determining unapparent or "hidden" losses caused by the impacts of pesticides. These are called externalities, and are covered below as well. Their economic impact can be greater than expected.

Soil Contamination

The use of pesticides and their accumulation in the soil can kill and severely reduce the essential soil macro- and microorganisms, including earthworms, insects, spiders, mites, fungi, essential mycorrhizae, and bacteria, thus reducing or stopping important nutrient cycling. Accidental spills on soil, which are usually associated with pesticide mixing and loading operations, can result in localized but severe soil contamination if not contained and dealt with rapidly and adequately.

Effects on Surface and Ground Water

The intense use of pesticides in agriculture or disease vector management can lead to the contamination of surface and ground water. Water runoff resulting from heavy rainfall can transport pesticides and their toxic metabolites to distant places located downstream, contaminating lakes, lagoons, reservoirs, ponds, and estuaries, and adversely affecting aquatic organisms. Discarding pesticides, washing spray equipment, or rinsing empty pesticide containers in or near streams and rivers can cause similar damage.

Pesticide Drift

When pesticide is being sprayed, poor aim or a light breeze can cause it to drift away from its intended target. Insecticide drift can be deadly to non-target organisms, including beneficial insects, spiders and mites. Pesticide drift can also expose people to risks associated with such chemicals. Spraying against the wind can poison the person applying the pesticide. Similarly, drifting herbicide can damage non-target crops and native vegetation within reach.

Effects on Non-target Organisms

Broad-spectrum insecticides not only destroy target insect pests but also destroy the predators and parasitoids that feed naturally on them. Pollinators and insect pests' natural enemies (parasitoids and predators) are especially vulnerable to pesticides—often more so than the pests. Most pesticides are also highly toxic to birds, fish, lizards, snakes, frogs, toads and other arthropods.

Disruption of Natural Control

By eliminating pests' natural enemies, excessive insecticide use can exacerbate pest problems and create new ones. Without natural enemies to keep them in check, pest populations can recover faster from the effects of a pesticide application than they could have in the presence of healthy natural enemies. This effect is known as pest resurgence. Again, many species that feed on crop plants are normally not a problem because their natural enemies keep their numbers relatively low. Intensive pesticide use, however, can eliminate these natural enemies, triggering a population explosion among their prey. Species that were merely potential pests or secondary pests may rise to "key pest" status as a result.

Pesticide Resistance

The development of genetic resistance to pesticides in pest organisms is another adverse consequence of pesticide overuse. Through 1990, at least 504 species of insects and mites, 150 species of pathogens, 273 weed species, 2 species of nematodes, and the Norway rat had developed resistance to at least one pesticide.

Externalities: Accounting for Economic Costs of Human Health and Environmental Impact

Externalities are the hidden costs associated with pesticide use, such as lost productivity due to chronic pesticide poisoning and lost ecosystem services such as the activity of natural enemies against pests. Unless these costs are accounted for, the cost to society for the reliance on chemical intensification to increase productivity will be under-recognized. Groundbreaking work on rice in the Philippines showed that when the health costs arising from pesticide exposure are included in the production budget, the most efficient and profitable pest management strategy can be natural control.

Factors That Lead to Risks to Human Health

African Production and Pesticide Use

Use of pesticides in Africa is lower than in other parts of the developing world. For comparison, in parts of Latin America, 90 percent or more of farmers raising a variety of crops use synthetic pesticides. Use in Africa is nowhere near this high, but it is increasing. Where African farmers wish to focus on one silver bullet that will solve their pest problems and can afford pesticides, use is high. The reasons are simple: synthetic pesticides appear to them to be fast, effective, and relatively easy to obtain. The pesticides marketed for farmer use are relatively simple to use, are culturally acceptable, and reduce yield losses to pests over the short term.

However, in Africa, smallholder farmers and many ministry of agriculture officials do not know how to calibrate or use sprayers properly, most farmers do not use safety equipment, recommendations given during safe use pesticide training are not followed, and well-written national regulations are never enforced. Moreover, donors and their implementing partners often do not have the resources to constantly monitor pesticide use schemes to ensure compliance with prescribed regulations and safe use. These problems are outlined below, and are being addressed by USAID programs through initiatives such as the Pesticide Evaluation Reports and Safer Use Action Plan (PERSUAP), described later.

Poor Pesticide Manufacturing Quality Control

Almost a third of the pesticides sold in developing countries are of poor quality. They may contain dangerous impurities, pesticide chemical breakdown products that are much more toxic than the active ingredient, and/or excessively high concentrations of active ingredients.

Poor Use and Dangerous Practices

Damage done by synthetic pesticides in Africa is compounded by the way they are used. Synthetic pesticides are intended to be used by trained applicators. The specific pesticide to be used against an identified pest is applied using specially designed machinery, equipment and clothing to protect the applicator. Guidelines are provided on quantity, frequency and timing of application relative to harvest, and these must be followed closely. In Africa, few if any of these procedural controls are adhered to with care by many smallholder farmers, although they are used by more educated larger-holder farmers.

Further, because of economic and educational conditions, smallholder farmers often view the "safe use" paradigm at best a waste of time and at worst a dangerous myth, and they do not appreciate the externalities listed above. Thus smallholders do not and probably will not follow "safe handling" practices even when these practices are taught to them. In addition, they often apply pesticides in excessive quantities, thinking that more is better.

Use of Very Dangerous New Pesticides

Organophosphates, carbamates, and phenylpyrazoles, three families of broad-spectrum pesticides are among the pesticides smallholders most frequently mention using. All of these can cause acute and chronic neurological damage, among other maladies. The World Health Organization has classified some of these insecticides, such as methamidophos and methyl parathion, as extremely or highly hazardous (Class I).

Use of Very Dangerous Old Pesticides

Banned synthetic pesticides, such as DDT, dieldrin, aldrin and other so-called chlorinated hydrocarbon pesticides, and pesticides of poor quality are often easy and cheap to produce and are frequently sold, legally and illegally, in developing countries. All farmers tend to use these older pesticides because they are generally cheaper and more potent, and they work well against a broader spectrum of pests. However, larger-holder farmers focusing on international trade will avoid these, due to developed-country restrictions.

Production and Use of Homemade Botanical Pesticide Concoctions

Although it is rare, NGO and USAID project managers may, while doing assessments of farmer's own IPM tools prior to project design, find a few smallholder farmers who are using combinations of "natural" products, such as tobacco extracts concocted with other types of plant extracts, that are actually quite toxic to people as well as pests. There are no US Environmental Protection Agency (and thus no USAID) regulations governing the use of many homemade botanical pesticide concoctions. Thus, many of these may not be promoted in a USAID-funded program, and farmers should be cautioned and encouraged to explore alternatives.

Local Government Policies

Inadequate local policies, regulation, and enforcement pertaining to the manufacture, import, formulation, packaging, labeling, transport, storage, sale, handling, application, and disposal of pesticides and their empty containers contribute to the increasing environmental and especially health risks associated with pesticide use in developing countries.

Dangers Across the Pesticide Cycle

Synthetic pesticides pose hazards not only to farmers and farm workers, but also to the health of others and to the environment at several stages in their life cycle:

- manufacturing
- transport, storage and application
- consumption of residues in food
- final disposal of outdated stocks

Hazards at each of these stages must be mitigated ... and are the responsibility of the group that orders the pesticide.

Factors That Lead to Risks to Environmental Diversity

Traditional mixed cropping systems, with their wide plant diversity, contain the conditions and resources (refuges, pollen, honey, hosts and prey) needed to support diversified natural enemy populations, which, in turn, contribute to keep populations of plant-feeding species from reaching damaging levels. Several factors discussed below, in addition to those listed above, stimulate overuse of pesticides, leading to environmental contamination.

Monoculture Plantings

The introduction of unsuitable crops, cropping systems, and crop-management practices can negatively affect the ecological balance of diverse and stable agro-ecosystems in sub-Saharan Africa. Larger-holder monoculture plantings provide pests with an easily accessible, vast and continuous source of food and shelter in time and space, and are generally predator-free. For instance, cotton grown as a monoculture tends to develop serious pest problems and an increasing dependence on chemical control within a few seasons. Rice and wheat, grown as monocultures, are subject to intense competition from weeds and often require at least one herbicide application per season.

The shift from low-input, highly diversified cropping systems to high-input, large-scale monocultures can exacerbate pest problems in several ways. In addition to the detrimental effects that pesticides have on pests' natural enemies, the introduction of monocultures of itself often results in a loss of natural enemy diversity.

Irrigated Production

The introduction of irrigation, primarily by larger-holders, allows crops to be grown year round but also allows some pests to survive and thrive throughout the year, as a new source of food and shelter becomes available during the dry season. These unforeseen pest problems can often lead to increased pesticide use and adverse health, environmental, and economic effects.

Bioaccumulation of Pesticides

In some cases, very serious broader or unexpected effects have come to light many years after the introduction of certain inadequately tested pesticides. DDT is perhaps the most famous example. DDT was found to build up or bio-accumulate in the food chain and to have unexpected reproductive and toxic effects, especially in certain predatory bird species.

Factors That Lead to Risks to Both Human Health and Environmental Diversity

Obsolete Pesticides

Currently, African countries store an enormous quantity (120,000 tons!) of old pesticides that came from many sources, including donors, the UN Food and Agriculture Organization (FAO), regional development banks and self-purchase by farmers. Many of these now unusable and degraded pesticides were donated for emergency programs against plagues of locusts, grasshoppers, armyworms, rodents, birds, mosquitoes, ticks, tsetse flies, and other disease vectors. Many of these are not being properly stored. Old deteriorating pesticide barrels leak, non-experts such as children have access to them, streams flow nearby, and some being sold by unscrupulous or unknowing crop protection agents for use.

Pesticides often degrade into chemical compounds even more dangerous and toxic than the original pesticide. Be aware of this and beware of allowing the use of these old pesticides in an IPM program. In fact, strongly discourage their use for any purpose.

Pest Resistance and a Cycle of Increased Use

When synthetic pesticides are used, a number of naturally resistant members of the pest organism population will survive. Since resistant organisms are the only survivors, the next generation of pests will be more resistant to the pesticide overall than the previous one was. Thus using synthetic pesticides creates a cycle where farmers must use greater and greater quantities of pesticides or turn to new pesticides to control the pest, often at greater expense and/or risk.

Little Known about the Biology and Ecology of Many Microscopic Pests

Pests that cannot be seen, such as viruses and bacteria, or insects that live in hidden habitats during the day and feed at night, are generally unrecognized or misunderstood, except by larger-holder farmers who may have been trained. This lack of knowledge can lead to misuse of pesticides. For instance, some farmers in Latin America have been known to use fungicides against viral or bacterial infections, due to misdiagnosis and/or poor advice.

Market Aesthetic Quality Requirements

High-value crops grown by larger-holders for export, including vegetables, fruits, and cut flowers, are often highly susceptible to pests, yet have high quality requirements imposed by the market. As a consequence, such crops tend to be treated with pesticides more frequently than crops grown for domestic consumption, leading to increased human and environmental dangers. It is not unusual, in such cases, for pest problems to worsen due to pesticide overuse. Farmers then feel compelled to spray more and more often, thus perpetuating and magnifying this unfortunate cycle.

[...]

"Mosquitoes are an important part of the food chain ... but the few species that carry disease can be a human health risk ... With proper surveillance and foresight, we can use only the pesticides that are absolutely necessary to control outbreaks of mosquito-borne diseases."

Pesticides Protect Humans from Disease-Carrying Pests

OARS, Inc.

In the following viewpoint, OARS explains how to use pesticides to prevent mosquito-borne diseases. The viewpoint states that mosquitos can carry diseases that are a risk to human health, but by reducing mosquito populations, outbreaks of disease can be controlled. Created in 1986, OARS is a 501(c)(3) non-profit organization dedicated to the conservation of the Assabet, Sudbury, and Concord Rivers. For the sake of public recreation, water supply, and wildlife habitats, OARS works to preserve and improve the rivers, their tributaries, and watersheds.

"Using Pesticides to Prevent Mosquito-borne Diseases," OARS, Inc. Reprinted by permission.

As you read, consider the following questions:

1. According to the viewpoint, what are the drawbacks to using pesticides on local mosquito populations?
2. What was problematic about older types of adulticides like DDT?
3. According to the viewpoint, what could be done to make public health the focus of mosquito control projects?

Carefully targeting the type and timing of pesticide applications can reduce the risks to the local ecology by limiting the total exposure to pesticides. Using chemicals that break down quickly so they do not persist in the environment, avoiding times when beneficial insects are active, and targeting mosquito larvae will help us do more good than harm.

Larvicides

Mosquito eggs hatch in still water and mosquito larvae spend up to two weeks growing until they pupate and fly away. Larvicides are pesticides that are added directly to water to kill the larvae. The most common larvicides are bacteria: *Bacillus thuringiensis israelensis* (Bti) and *Bacillus sphaericus* make a toxin that kills the larvae when they eat the bacteria. The toxin is specific to mosquitoes and a few closely-related insects like black flies and midges, but is not toxic to bees or fish.

Bti can knock down mosquito breeding at an application site within 24 hours, but it must be applied directly to the water that larvae live in. It is available in briquettes (like Mosquito Dunks©) and powders for use in rain barrels and catch basins. Bti can be sprayed from a truck, but it will only be effective if it actually lands in the water. Bti is only effective for a short time, which is why slowly-dissolving briquettes are preferable. Spraying inaccessible wetlands from helicopters in the early spring has questionable effectiveness for disease control.

Growth regulators like methoprene (Altosid©) can also be used. Methoprene acts like a hormone and prevents mosquito larvae from developing into adults, but it has been shown to be toxic to amphibians and shellfish. Like Bti, methoprene is available in a briquette, so it is important to check the label to distinguish whether you are getting the bacteria-based larvicide or the more broadly toxic growth regulator. Methoprene lasts longer in the environment than Bti, which is why many communities use it in catch basins. Alternating bacteria and growth regulators can prevent the development of resistant larvae.

Adulticides

Adulticides, such as sumithrin (Anvil©), other pyrethroids, and malathion are very effective at killing flying insects, especially adult mosquitoes. But they also are toxic to bees, dragonflies, and fish. In high concentrations, they are also neurotoxic to human beings. Typically, adulticides are sprayed by handheld sprayers or trucks. When you see a truck spraying insecticide on a summer evening, it is most likely spraying an adulticide like sumithrin.

Previous generations of adulticides, like DDT, persisted in the environment and killed fish and birds, but modern adulticides break down fairly quickly in sunlight and do not become a persistent problem. Still, they are neurotoxins, and can affect fish, and in higher concentrations, birds and mammals. They should not be sprayed directly on water. To prevent pollinators from being harmed, mosquito adulticides are often sprayed after dusk when mosquitoes, but not bees, are active. However, some beneficial insects are active at night. Bees and other pollinating insects will be out at dawn landing on flowers that may have residue before the sun has broken it down.

Entomologist Dr. Anthony Kiszewski of Bentley University, questions whether spraying adulticides has a significant effect on the disease-carrying mosquito populations in Massachusetts: "These chemicals break down so quickly. They will only have an effect if a mosquito is actually touched by the chemical, and the trucks only have access to the spaces directly adjacent to the road."

The quick breakdown of pyrethroids means that they need to be sprayed between dusk and 11pm when mosquitoes are active. While that might have a small impact on the mosquitoes that carry EEE and West Nile, the *Aedes* mosquitoes that carry Zika are most active during the day so they would be less affected. Even when the local adult population is reduced, new mosquitoes will hatch within days.

Mosquito Control Projects

Most towns do not have the resources to assess when there is a public health need to control mosquitoes. The Mass. Dept. of Agricultural Resources oversees mosquito surveillance programs in districts across the state. Individual towns join their local Mosquito Control Project, which monitors mosquitoes, maintains ditches, and educates the public. The Control Projects also apply pesticides: adding larvicide to catch basins, doing aerial spraying with larvicides over waterways that have been identified as mosquito breeding grounds, and sending out trucks to spray adulticides.

Surveillance programs collect mosquitoes in member towns with CO_2-baited traps, and identify the number and species collected. This is particularly important since most of the mosquito species in Massachusetts do not cause disease. The program also identifies mosquito breeding grounds, and interfaces with the DPH to identify disease presence in mosquito populations. Surveillance can help distinguish between mosquitoes that harbor arbovirus (mosquito-borne virus) and innocuous species that are just a nuisance.

Mass Audubon Senior Policy Analyst Heidi Ricci points out that, "One of the biggest flaws in the state mosquito control system is that communities can't get mosquito testing services unless they are part of a district, but then they often are forced to sign on to a program that allows homeowners to request neighborhood spraying based on an individual's perception of mosquito nuisance." Members of the Central Mass. Mosquito Control Project do not get to pick which services they get. The Project applies larvicides in catch basins early in the season, and decides when adulticides will be applied. A detailed adulticide spraying schedule is published on the Project's website.

However, not all projects operate by the same rules. East Middlesex Mosquito Control Project (EMMCP) superintendent Dr. David Henley points out that his Project provides more flexible services, allowing members to select whether they want only larvicides or, at a greater cost, comprehensive adulticide applications. Dr. Kiszewski, the Concord EMMCP representative, points out that Concord has limited its pesticide use to larvicides in catch basins and mosquito breeding sites. But Concord's restraint is just one end of the pest management spectrum. According to the EMMCP website, Sudbury and Bedford were sprayed with sumithrin this summer.

Environmentalists like Ms. Ricci would like to see public health be the focus of the mosquito control projects. This could be facilitated by adding representatives from the Departments of Public Health and Fisheries and Wildlife to the control project management, and adding local public health official representation to the regional districts. Surveillance could be expanded to look for impacts of pesticide use on wildlife, especially pollinators, fish, and birds. Management techniques should be continually updated to incorporate the best scientifically-validated methods.

In the meantime, it is up to individuals to support the most environmentally-friendly practices in their own towns by making their opinions known to their town representative. Homeowners who wish to opt out of pesticide applications must file an on-line request with the Mass. Department of Agricultural Resources, and mark their property with white plastic or aluminum pie plates of at least 9 inches diameter, with "No Spray" written in permanent marker, in easily visible locations at least every 50 feet along the property adjacent to the road. During a public health emergency it is unlikely that an individual homeowner will be able to opt out of spraying.

Homeowners can contract with pest control companies to spray pesticides on their property, but buyer beware: you pay these companies to apply chemicals, not prevent disease. They may plan to apply pesticides when it is convenient, not when mosquitoes are active. And their treatment may not distinguish the disease-carrying mosquitoes from the nuisance of the many disease-free mosquito species. Pesticides that are over-used can also lead to pesticide resistance.

| "With every new insecticide
| introduction ... cases of resistance
| surfaced 2 to 20 years later."

Pesticides Make It Harder to Kill Disease-Carrying Pests

Insecticide Resistance Action Committee

In the following excerpted viewpoint, the Insecticide Resistance Action Committee (IRAC) argues that due to the development of resistance, widespread pesticide use is no longer effective for pest control and instead escalates the issue in an aggressive cycle. Rather than liberally using pesticides, the IRAC encourages growers to utilize appropriate management techniques to combat insecticide resistance. Established in 1984, the IRAC functions as a specialist technical group of the trade association CropLife to provide a coordinated industry response to the development of insect resistance.

As you read, consider the following questions:

1. According to the viewpoint, what is responsible for the rapid buildup of resistance in most insects?
2. According to the viewpoint, what is the best strategy for avoiding resistance?
3. According to the viewpoint, what must happen for insecticide resistance management to succeed?

"Resistance: The Facts—History and Overview of Resistance," Insecticide Resistance Action Committee (IRAC). Reprinted by permission.

R esistance to insecticides was first documented in 1914 by A.L. Melander in the *Journal of Economic Entomology*. He described scale insects, still alive, under a "crust of dried spray" of an inorganic insecticide. Between 1914 and 1946, another 11 cases of resistance to inorganic pesticides were recorded.

Then came development of organic insecticides, such as DDT, and the agricultural industry breathed a sigh of relief, believing that insecticide resistance was an issue of the past. Unfortunately, that feeling of relief quickly faded—by 1947, housefly resistance to DDT was documented. With every new insecticide introduction— cyclodienes, carbamates, formamidines, organophosphates, pyrethroids, even *Bacillus thuringiensis*—cases of resistance surfaced 2 to 20 years later.

This phenomenon is described by some as the "pesticide treadmill." A rise in an insect population causes damage to a commodity; growers respond by attacking the pests with a product to reduce the damage; the pests become resistant to the chemical and the resistant strain is not controlled, which leads to the application of more chemicals. Insecticide resistance climbs, problems increase, more product is applied; eventually growers switch to another pesticide (if one is available) and the vicious cycle continues.

Genetics and intensive application of pesticides are responsible for the quick buildup of resistance in most insects and mites. Natural selection by an insecticide allows some insects with resistance genes to survive and pass the resistance trait on to their offspring. The percentage of resistant insects in a population continues to multiply while susceptible ones are eliminated by the insecticide.

Eventually, resistant insects outnumber susceptible ones and the pesticide is no longer effective. How quickly resistance develops depends on several factors, including how quickly the insects reproduce, the migration and host range of the pest, the crop protection product's persistence and specificity, and the rate, timing and number of applications made. Resistance increases fastest in situations such as greenhouses, where insects or mites reproduce quickly, there is little or no immigration of susceptible individuals, and the grower may spray frequently.

Resistance Is Costly; Management Is Economical

It has been estimated that insecticide resistance in the United States adds $40 million to the total insecticide bill in additional treatment costs or alternative controls. Better management of pesticides by farmers and the crop experts assisting them, industry specialists say, could reduce this bill and lead to more effective, more efficient use of products.

Consider, for example, that resistance in the Colorado potato beetle (*Leptinotarsa decemlineata*) cost Michigan potato producers $16 million in crop losses in 1991. And, failed cotton production due to resistance in the budworm/bollworm pest complex in India, Thailand, and Mexico collapsed the economics of entire communities.

Despite this, insecticides and miticides are still among the most efficient tools for keeping pest populations under control. Managing pesticides to avoid resistance development is vital to sustainable production of commodities.

What Causes Resistance?

Resistance is a heritable change in the sensitivity of a pest population that is reflected in the repeated failure of an insecticide to achieve the expected level of control when used according to the label recommendation for that pest species. Natural genetic variation in insect populations can allow some individuals to survive an insecticide treatment. Typically, individuals carrying resistance gene(s) are very rare, but after insecticide application, resistant individuals are among the few individuals to survive the treatment. These surviving individuals then potentially pass the gene(s) responsible for the insecticide resistance to their offspring. The repeated use of the same insecticide or another insecticide with the same mode of action (MoA) increases the frequency of these resistant individuals until the resistant population replaces the susceptible population and the insecticide is no longer able to adequately control the pest population. The speed with which resistance develops depends on several factors, including how fast the insects reproduce, the migration and host range of the pest, exposure to nearby susceptible populations, the persistence and specificity of the insecticide product, and the rate, timing and number of applications made. Resistance increases fastest in situations such as greenhouses, where insects or mites reproduce quickly, there is little or no immigration of susceptible individuals and the user may spray frequently.

Insects develop resistance to insecticides in multiple ways, which involves physiological and behavioral changes that protect insects from the chemicals conferring resistance. Mechanisms of insect/mite resistance often utilize more than one of these mechanisms at the same time.

Metabolic Resistance

Insects use their internal enzyme systems to break down insecticides. Resistant strains may possess greater levels or more efficient forms of these enzymes. In addition to being more efficient, these enzyme systems also may be broad spectrum, meaning they can degrade many different pesticides.

The earliest reported case of metabolic resistance was DDT-resistant houseflies.vResistance to organophosphates (e.g., carbamates, acylureas) and other insecticide classes can also be affected by metabolic resistance. If metabolic resistance is suspected, it can be confirmed in a laboratory.

Rotating to a different compound to combat resistance is likely to help only if the second compound is metabolized by different enzyme systems within the target pest.

Altered Target-site Resistance

Altered target-site resistance is caused by a change in the structure of the site or the number of sites where the pesticide causes toxicity to the insect and has been shown for several chemical classes. Changes in insect target sites have been found in several species, including tobacco budworm (*Heliothis virescens*) and the Colorado potato beetle (*Leptinotarsa decemlineata*).

Identifying this form of resistance can be done in the laboratory. Resistance management can be practiced by using different classes of compounds that target different sites; for example, rotating between carbamates and pyrethroids.

Penetration Resistance

Penetration resistance occurs when insects, such as the housefly (*Musca domestica*), can slow absorption of chemicals into their bodies because their outer cuticle has developed barriers against the products. The bad news is that this can protect insects from a wide range of insecticides.

Penetration resistance is usually present along with other forms of resistance, and reduced penetration intensifies the effects of those other mechanisms. Penetration resistance must be diagnosed in a laboratory, and specialists advise alternating or rotating insecticides from different classes to combat penetration resistance.

Behavioral Resistance

Behavioral resistance occurs when insects or mites are able to evade contact with insecticides through avoidance. This mechanism of resistance has been reported for several classes of insecticides, including organochlorines, organophosphates, carbamates and pyrethroids.

Insects may simply quit feeding if they come across certain insecticides, or leave the area where spraying occurred (i.e., move to underside of a sprayed leaf, move deeper in crop canopy or fly away from the target area). With transgenic plants, insects may stop short of consuming or eating enough toxin to kill them. Behavioral resistance is hard to diagnose.

What Can You Do About Resistance?

We've now covered the background information on insecticide resistance. You know the basics on what it is, how it develops, what it can cost growers, and what forms it takes. The following sections should help you explain to growers how to delay or prevent resistance development on their farms, how to determine whether it is present, and how to manage it if it does become a problem in their operation.

An integrated approach prevents resistance. The ultimate strategy to avoid insecticide resistance is prevention. More and more crop specialists recommend insecticide resistance management programs as one part of a larger integrated pest management (IPM) approach. Insecticide resistance management, a major IPM strategy, involves three basic components: monitoring pest complexes for population density and trends, focusing on economic injury levels and integrating control strategies.

Monitoring pests. Scouting is one of the key activities producers can implement as part of their insecticide resistance management strategy. Farmers should follow progress of insect population development in their fields (with or without the assistance of a crop consultant or advisor) to determine if and when control measures are warranted. They should monitor and consider natural enemies when making control decisions. After treatment, they should continue monitoring to assess pest populations and control.

Focus on economic thresholds. Insecticides should be used only if insects are numerous enough to cause economic losses that exceed the cost of the insecticide plus application. An exception might be in-furrow, at-planting treatments for early season pests that usually reach damaging levels annually. Encourage farmers to consult their local advisors about economic thresholds of target pests in their areas.

Integrating control strategies. Monitoring is just one element of an insecticide resistance management (IRM) program. It is important to follow an integrated approach.

- Incorporate as many different control mechanisms as possible. IPM-based programs can include the use of synthetic insecticides, biological insecticides, beneficial insects (predator/parasites), cultural practices, transgenic plants, crop rotation, pest-resistant crop varieties and chemical attractants or deterrents. Select insecticides with care and consider the impact on future pest populations. Even cultural practices, such as destroying overwintering areas, can play a role in managing resistance.

- Time applications carefully. Time insecticide and miticide applications against the most vulnerable life stage of the insect pest. Use spray rates and application intervals recommended by the manufacturer.

- Mix and apply carefully. As resistance increases, the margin for error in terms of insecticide dose, timing, coverage, etc., assumes even greater importance. In the case of aerial application, the swath widths should be marked, preferably by permanent markers. Sprayer nozzles should be checked for blockage and wear and be able to handle pressure adequate for good coverage. Spray equipment should be properly calibrated and checked on a regular basis. Also, in tree fruits, proper and intense pruning will allow better canopy penetration and tree coverage. Use application volumes and techniques recommended by the manufacturers and local advisors.

- Protect beneficials. Select insecticides in a manner that causes minimum damage to populations of beneficial arthropods.

- Preserve susceptible genes. Some programs try to preserve susceptible individuals within the target population by providing a haven for susceptible insects, such as unsprayed areas within treated fields, adjacent "refuge" fields, or habitat attractions within a treated field that facilitate immigration. These susceptible individuals may outcompete and interbreed with resistant individuals, diluting the impact of resistance.

- Consider crop residue options. Destroying crop residue can deprive insects of food and overwintering sites. This cultural practice will kill pesticide-resistant pests (as well as susceptible ones) and prevent them from producing resistant offspring for the next season. However, farmers should review their soil conservation requirements before removing residue.

[...]

If Resistance Is Suspected

If growers encounter control failure and suspect they have a case of insecticide resistance, it's best not to jump to any conclusions until they consult with crop specialists. Several other problems have similar symptoms, so if poor control is experienced, growers should first check for:

- Application error. Were the timing of the application and the dosage correct? Were proper product carriers used? Was the correct application method followed? Was the timing for treatment evaluation incorrect, or does the product require more than one application?
- Equipment failure. Were the spray nozzles blocked? Were all parts of the applicator functioning properly? Was the equipment calibrated for accurate application using recommended spray volumes and pressures?
- Environmental conditions. Did rain or overhead irrigation occur too soon after application? Were temperature, wind or other environmental conditions less than ideal for application?

Be Certain It's Resistance

If resistance is suspected, there are several steps growers can take to keep the problem from mushrooming. First and foremost, they should not respray with an insecticide of the same chemical class. Their crop protection sales agent should be contacted to help evaluate the cause of control failure. He or she will call additional experts as needed to accurately confirm insecticide resistance.

Confirming Resistance

Reliable data on resistance, rather than anecdotal reports or assumptions, is the cornerstone of successful resistance management and key to this is the availability of sound baseline data on the susceptibility of the target pest to the toxicant. A large number of bioassay and biochemical tests are used to characterize resistance, but they are not necessarily comparable because different parameters and criteria are used. IRAC has evaluated, validated and published a wide range of standard resistance testing methods and these are freely available on the IRAC website. Importantly, they provide consistent and comparable methods for evaluating the status of resistance in insect populations, and a means of assessing the success of IRM strategies. Most of these methods require only basic equipment and are suitable for use in laboratories worldwide.

[...]

Resistance Management for Biotechnology-Derived Insect-Protected Crops

Since their introduction, growers have rapidly adopted biotechnology-derived crops that have been improved to express proteins for insect control, because these crops provide excellent protection from key damaging insect pests. By protecting yields against insect pests, these crops offer superior environment and health benefits, while benefiting farmer livelihoods. It is important that stewardship and management programs are in place that effectively delay the evolution of resistance in target pest populations to these crops, while enabling the benefits of the technology to the environment and to agriculture to be realized.

Insect resistance management plans need to be suitable for the given production situation. What works for large monoculture production systems in North and South America is unlikely to be appropriate for the small, more diverse agriculture of Southeast Asia or Africa. The technical data and practical experience accumulated by developers, researchers and growers with insect protected crops in many global regions can inform different aspects of resistance management leading to robust, science-based IRM plans.

The Use of Refuges

Refuges contain crop plants without a biotech trait for protection against the target insects and provide an area where susceptible insects can thrive. This area serves to dilute selection pressure for resistance. In the case of a "high dose" trait, the susceptible insects produced by the refuge area additionally serve to mate with any rare resistant insects surviving in the insect protected crop area. This prevents inheritance by the progeny of resistance to the control protein. The size of the structured refuge area must take into account the factors that affect the selection pressure for resistance, as well as grower acceptance. Refuge areas typically yield less than their biotech counterparts because they must sustain some level of insect damage to produce susceptible insects. The value of the crop and the level of industrialization of the agricultural system (versus subsistence farming) must be taken into account when determining appropriate refuge sizes. The ideal size for refuges also depends on the target pest and crop. Refer to the seed suppliers' recommendations for more specific information.

In many situations, it is most desirable for the refuge to be planted as a separate block, or in a separate field from the insect protected crop. This isolation prevents wandering insects from sampling insect protected and non-insect protected plants thereby receiving less than the full insecticidal dose. Cross over of insects from protected to refuge crops or vice versa, can reduce the effective refuge size and can favor the survival of partially-resistant insects. With a separate refuge, the grower is responsible for ensuring the refuge is planted alongside the insect protected variety. Such a separate refuge can be provided by supplying a small package of refuge seed along with the larger amount of biotech-derived seed, or by encouraging the grower to separately purchase refuge seed.

In other situations, it can be more desirable for the refuge to be provided as a seed blend. This simplifies the grower's operations and shifts the onus of compliance with refuge requirements to the seed provider. In cases where insect movement among plants is limited, or where the movement doesn't favor survival of partially-resistant insects, seed blends may be highly effective.

[...]

Out of Money, Out of Time

General insecticide use is no longer the only answer to pest control. Insects have developed widespread, insecticide-defeating resistance to some of the traditional treatments, and the industry may not have enough resources to continually develop and supply the market with new products precisely when needed to replace old ones. Growers with resistance problems do not have enough time to wait for new chemistry. It is imperative that the effectiveness of available insecticides be conserved by growers through adoption of these management principles. By working together, insecticide resistance can be managed!

Periodical and Internet Sources Bibliography

The following articles have been selected to supplement the diverse views presented in this chapter.

Tom Atwell, "Pesticides May Get Rid of Ticks, But at What Cost?" *Portland Press Herald*, January 3, 2016. https://www.pressherald. com/2016/01/03/the-pesticides-bifenthrin-and-permethrin-may-get-rid-of-ticks-but-at-what-cost/

Julie Beck, "Pesticides Aren't the Best Way to Fight Zika-Carrying Mosquitoes," *The Atlantic,* December 9, 2016. https://www. theatlantic.com/health/archive/2016/12/pesticides-arent-the-best-way-to-fight-zika-carrying-mosquitoes/510167/

Jennifer Hsaio, "GMOs and Pesticides: Helpful or Harmful?" Science in the News, August 10, 2015. http://sitn.hms.harvard.edu/ flash/2015/gmos-and-pesticides/

Donald G. McNeil Jr., "Laced with Two Insecticides, New Nets Protect Children From Malaria," *New York Times*, May 4, 2018. https://www.nytimes.com/2018/05/04/health/malaria-nets-children-africa.html?rref=collection%2Ftimestopic%2FPesticides

Kevin Rushby, "The British Countryside Is Being Killed by Herbicides and Insecticides—Can Anything Save It?" *Guardian,* May 31, 2018. https://www.theguardian.com/uk-news/2018/may/31/ herbicides-insecticides-save-british-countryside-meaows

Roger Schlueter, "Are Pesticides Safe to Use on Fruit and Vegetables? The Debate Continues," *Belleville News-Democrat*, April 25, 2017. http://www.bnd.com/living/liv-columns-blogs/answer-man/ article146700949.html

Erik Stokstad, "Pesticides Found in Honey Around the World," *Science*, October 5, 2018. http://www.sciencemag.org/ news/2017/10/pesticides-found-honey-around-world

Holly Yan, Shawn Nottingham, and AnneClaire Stapleton, "Texas Pesticide Deaths: Chemical May Have Sickened, but Cleanup Was Fatal," *CNN*, January 3, 2017. https://www.cnn.com/2017/01/03/ health/texas-pesticide-deaths/index.html

CHAPTER 2

How Do Pesticides and GMOs Affect the Agriculture Industry?

Chapter Preface

As industrialized farming models become more intensive, modern agriculture is being faced with growing environmental damage from the excessive use of pesticides and the high-tech farming practices used for GM crops. More than 80 percent of the corn grown in the United States is genetically engineered to be equipped with two genes: one that kills the insects that eat its seed, and one that enables it to withstand glyphosate, a common herbicide found in weed killers. This is significant because when crops are able to withstand herbicides, farmers are able to save on labor costs by quickly dousing entire fields with herbicides.

The widespread adoption of the GM corn seed has led to a decrease in insecticide use, but at the same time, herbicide use has been increasing. This is due to pesticide resistance—the more herbicides are used, the more weeds will gradually build up a resistance that requires even more herbicide to defeat. This cycle has resulted in copious amounts of pesticide being used to treat the epidemic of superweeds, an action that has in turn harmed the environment with large deposits of chemicals contaminating the soil, air, and water.

At the same time, agricultural sustainability and expansion is being threatened by industrial practices like specialized production and crop monocultures. Such practices strip diversity away from agroecosystems, ruining the soil and making crops dependent on chemicals, but as this system is profitable to farmers and enables them to serve global markets, the trend continues.

The following chapter examines issues of agrochemical farming and considers ways to develop more sustainable practices and better environmental conservation.

"*The specialization of farms has led to the image that agriculture is a modern miracle of food production. However, excessive reliance on farm specialization (including crop monocultures) and inputs such as capital-intensive technology, pesticides, and synthetic fertilizers, have negatively impacted the environment and rural society.*"

Pesticides and Modern Crop Practices Accelerate Agricultural Damage

Miguel A. Altieri and Clara Ines Nicholls

In the following viewpoint, Miguel A. Altieri and Clara Ines Nicholls argue that the practices of modern agriculture have serious ecological impacts and that existing food production systems are not sustainable in the long-term. The authors claim that overreliance on farm specialization and monocultures have resulted in "ecological diseases" that plague the environment, such as loss of soil productivity and croplands, pollution, and destruction of natural control mechanisms. Altieri and Nicholls are agronomists and professors of agroecology at the University of California, Berkeley.

"Ecological Impacts of Modern Agriculture in the United States and Latin America," by Miguel A. Altieri and Clara Ines Nicholls, David Rockefeller Center Series on Latin American Studies, Harvard University Press. Reprinted by permission.

As you read, consider the following questions:

1. According to the viewpoint, why are farms becoming less diverse and what kind of negative effects does this have?
2. According to the viewpoint, what factors have allowed for the transition toward specialization and monocultures?
3. According to the viewpoint, why is natural resource degradation not only an ecological process?

During the last two decades, interest in sustainable agriculture has grown to worldwide proportions, with various sectors of society slowly realizing that agrochemical technologies, resource scarcity, environmental degradation, uncontrolled economic growth, etc., are seriously threatening the long-term limits of agricultural expansion. Although these problems affect most regions in the world, their intensity or perceived importance differs in each area, as does the motivation behind the pursuit of sustainable agricultural development. Clearly, in industrialized countries (ICs) a major factor has been the need to deal with the consequences of technology-induced environmental degradation resulting from a sort of "development oversaturation." Conversely, in developing countries (LDCs), although IC's environmental problems are common in commercial agricultural areas, historically speaking, "development" has not reached the vast population of resource-poor farmers. Therefore, there is a great need to match agricultural development with the needs of this large and impoverished sector of society (Redclift 1989).

Today, numerous agricultural scientists agree that modern agriculture confronts an environmental crisis. A growing number of people have become concerned about the long-term sustainability of existing food production systems (Conway and Pretty 1991). Evidence has accumulated showing that whereas the present capital and technology-intensive farming systems have been extremely productive and able to furnish low-cost food, they also bring a variety of economic, environmental and social problems (Audirac 1997).

Evidence also shows that the very nature of the agricultural structure and prevailing policies in a capitalist setting have led to an environmental crisis by favoring large farm size, specialized production, crop monocultures and mechanization. Today as more and more farmers are integrated into international economies, the biological imperative of diversity disappears due to the use of many kinds of pesticides and synthetic fertilizers, and specialized farms are rewarded by economies of scale (Pretty 1995). In turn, lack of rotations and diversification take away key self-regulating mechanisms, turning monocultures into highly vulnerable agroecosystems dependent on high chemical inputs (Gliessman 1997).

The expansion of farm specialization and monocultures has increased dramatically worldwide, where the same crop (usually corn, wheat, or rice) is grown year after year in the same field, or very simple rotations are used (such as corn-soybeans-corn-soybeans). Also, fields that in the past contained many different crops, or a single crop with a high degree of genetic variability, are now entirely devoted to a genetically uniform single crop (Vallve, 1993). Available data indicate that the amount of crop diversity per unit of arable land has decreased and that croplands have shown a tendency toward concentration. The conventional mode for industrial agriculture in Latin America, especially the so-called "Green Revolution" has emphasized the application of a reductionist scientific paradigm focusing on high yielding varieties (HYVs) that depend on purchased packages of chemical, mechanical and energy inputs. Yield maximization, uniformity of genetic resources and crop varieties, and simplification of farming systems have, for decades, driven technical innovation (Thrupp 1998). There are political and economic forces influencing the trend to devote large areas to monoculture, and in fact the economies of scale of such systems contribute significantly to the ability of national agriculture to serve international markets (McIsaac and Edwards 1994).

In Latin America, as countries are pulled into the existing international order and change policies in order to serve the unprecedented debt, governments increasingly embrace neoliberal economic models that promote export-led growth (Altieri and Masera 1993). Despite the fact that in some countries such as Argentina, Chile, and Mexico the model appears successful at the macroeconomic level, deforestation, soil erosion, industrial pollution, pesticide contamination and loss of biodiversity (including genetic erosion) proceed at alarming rates and are not reflected in the economic indicators. So far there is no clear system to account for the environmental costs of such development models (LACDE 1990).

The technologies allowing the shift toward specialization and monoculture have been mechanization, the improvement of crop varieties, and the development of agrochemicals to fertilize crops and control weeds, insects and other crop pests, as well as antibiotics and growth stimulants for agricultural animals. United States government commodity policies over the last several decades have encouraged the acceptance and utilization of these technologies (Buttel and Gertler 1982). And economic liberalization, open markets and reduction of trade barriers have all been forces triggering agricultural specialization in Latin America. In addition, the largest agribusiness corporations have found that concentrating certain processing facilities for a given product (chickens, hogs, or wheat) in specific countries produces more profits, which lead to more farm and regional specialization (Murray 1994).

The First Wave of Environmental Problems

The specialization of farms has led to the image that agriculture is a modern miracle of food production. However, excessive reliance on farm specialization (including crop monocultures) and inputs such as capital-intensive technology, pesticides, and synthetic fertilizers, have negatively impacted the environment and rural society. A number of what might be called "ecological diseases" have been associated with the intensification of food production.

There are problems directly associated with the basic resources of soil and water, which include soil erosion, loss of inherent soil productivity and depletion of nutrient reserves, salinization and alkalization (especially in arid and semi-arid regions), pollution of surface and groundwater, and loss of croplands to urban development. Problems directly related to crops, animals, and pests include loss of crop, wild plant, and animal genetic resources, elimination of natural enemies of pests, pest resurgence and genetic resistance to pesticides, chemical contamination, and destruction of natural control mechanisms (Conway and Pretty 1991). Each "ecological disease" is usually viewed as an independent problem, rather than what it really is—a symptom of a poorly designed and poorly functioning agroecosystem.

Under conditions of intensive management, treatment of such "ecological diseases" requires an increase in the external costs to the extent that, in some agricultural systems, the amount of energy invested to produce a desired yield surpasses the energy harvested. The substantial yield losses due to pests, about 20 to 30 percent for most crops despite the increase in the use of pesticides (about 4.7 billion pounds of pesticides were used worldwide in 1995, 1.2 billion pounds in the United States alone), is a symptom of the environmental crisis affecting agriculture (Pimentel and Lehman 1993).

Pesticides

Cultivated plants grown in genetically homogenous monocultures do not possess the necessary ecological defense mechanisms to tolerate the impact of pest outbreaks. Modern agriculturists have selected crops mainly for high yields and high palatability, making them more susceptible to pests by sacrificing natural resistance for productivity (Altieri 1995). As modern agricultural practices reduce or eliminate the resources and opportunities for natural enemies of pests, their numbers decline, decreasing the biological

How Do GM Crops Affect the Environment?

Transgenic crops may have indirect environmental effects as a result of changing agricultural or environmental practices associated with the new varieties. These indirect effects may be beneficial or harmful depending on the nature of the changes involved (ICSU, GM Science Review Panel). Scientists agree that the use of conventional agricultural pesticides and herbicides has damaged habitats for farmland birds, wild plants and insects and has seriously reduced their numbers (ICSU, GM Science Review Panel, Royal Society). Transgenic crops are changing chemical and land-use patterns and farming practices, but scientists do not fully agree whether the net effect of these changes will be positive or negative for the environment (ICSU). Scientists acknowledge that more comparative analysis of new technologies and current farming practices is needed.

"What Direct Effects Could Genetically Modified Plants Have on the Environment?" Food and Agriculture Organization of the United Nations.

suppression of pests. Due to this lack of natural controls, an investment of about $40 billion in pesticide control is incurred yearly by US farmers, which is estimated to save approximately $16 billion in US crops. However, the indirect costs of pesticide use to the environment and public health have to be balanced against these benefits. Based on the available data, the environmental costs (impacts on wildlife, pollinators, natural enemies, fisheries, water, and development of resistance) and social costs (human poisonings and illnesses) of pesticide use reach about $8 billion each year (Pimentel and Lehman 1993).

What is worrisome is that pesticide use is still high and still rising in some cropping systems. Data from California show that from 1991 to 1995 pesticide use increased from 161 to 212 million pounds of active ingredient. This increase was not due to increases in planted acreage, as statewide crop acreage remained constant during this period. Much of the increase was in particularly toxic pesticides, many of which are linked to cancers, used on such crops as strawberries and grapes (Liebman 1997).

In Latin America, pesticide use in general is increasing, especially in large scale production systems. Pesticide sales more than doubled in the region between 1976 and 1980 (IRL 1981), exceeding industry predictions (Farm Chemicals 1976). There was a continuous growth in consumption, both through importation and domestic production, throughout the 1980s. Latin America's share of the global pesticide market, currently around 10 percent, is steadily increasing. Brazil alone accounts for nearly 50 percent of the total sales in the region, followed by Mexico, Argentina, and Colombia. From 1980 to 1986, pesticide sales rose dramatically in Brazil and Argentina. If current trends continue, the cost to Latin America of chemical pest control is expected to reach US $3.97 billion by the year 2000 (Maltby 1980).

Such increased use of pesticides has had a heavy human toll. Self reported rates of pesticide intoxication from surveys in Latin America run at about 13 percent of agricultural workers per year. Pesticide poisonings among children under 18 years of age account for roughly 10–20 percent of all poisonings. Several studies conducted throughout the region alarmingly confirm the widespread risks that pesticide exposure inflicts on farmworkers and their families (McConnell et al. 1993).

Fertilizers

Fertilizers have been praised as being responsible for the temporary increase in food production observed in many countries. National average rates of nitrogen applied to most arable lands fluctuate between 120-550 kg N/ha. But increased fertilizer use is quickly approaching the point of diminishing yield returns. In the case of Chile in 1988 about 316 thousand tons of chemical fertilizers were used. In eight years, urea exhibited a 764 percent increase in use, mostly for application in cereals. Although between 1985–1990, wheat received 62 percent more fertilizer than in the previous decade, this resulted only in a 3.1 percent increase in yields (Altieri and Rojas 1994). This is a clear indication of yield leveling off and in some cases even declining despite the use of higher amounts of fertilizers. Such processes have been linked to fertilizer-induced soil degradation (McGuiness 1993).

The bountiful harvests created at least in part through the use of synthetic fertilizers have associated environmental costs. Two main reasons why synthetic fertilizers pollute the environment are their wasteful application and the fact that crops use them inefficiently. A significant amount of fertilizer that is not recovered by the crops ends up in surface or groundwater. Nitrate contamination of aquifers is widespread and in dangerously high levels in many rural regions of the world. It is estimated that more than 25 percent of the drinking water wells in the United States contain nitrogen in the nitrate form above the safety standard of 10 parts per million. Such nitrate levels are hazardous to human health, and studies have linked nitrate uptake to metahemoglobinemia (low blood oxygen levels) in children and to gastric, bladder, and esophageal cancers in adults (Conway and Pretty 1995).

It is estimated that about 50–70 percent of all nutrients that reach surface waters in the United States are derived from fertilizers. Fertilizer nutrients that enter surface waters (rivers, lakes, bays) can promote eutrophication, characterized usually by an explosion of algae. Algal blooms turn the water bright green, sometimes prevent light from penetrating beneath surface layers, and therefore kill plants living on the bottom. Such dead vegetation serves as food for other aquatic microorganisms, soon depleting water of its oxygen and inhibiting the decomposition of organic residues, which accumulate on the bottom (McGuiness 1993).

Eventually, such nutrient enrichment of freshwater ecosystems can lead to the destruction of all animal life in the water systems. In the Gulf of Mexico there is a huge "dead zone," extending from the mouth of the Mississippi River to the west, where the excessive nutrients from farmland are believed to be responsible for oxygen depletion. It is also believed that excess nutrients may stimulate populations of the very toxic form of Pfiesteria, an organism that kills fish and is harmful to humans (McGuiness 1993).

Synthetic nitrogen fertilizers can also become air pollutants and have recently been implicated in contributing to global warming and the destruction of the ozone layer. Their excessive use causes soils to become more acidic and also leads to nutritional imbalances in plants, resulting in a higher incidence of damage from insect pests and diseases (McGuiness 1993, Conway and Pretty 1995).

It is clear then that the first wave of environmental problems is deeply rooted in the prevalent socioeconomic system that promotes monocultures and the use of high-input technologies and agricultural practices that lead to natural resource degradation (Buttel and Gertler 1982). Such degradation is not only an ecological process, but also a social and political-economic process. Therefore, the problem of agricultural production cannot be regarded only as a technological one; attention to social, cultural, political, and economic issues that account for the crisis is crucial. This is particularly true today where the economic and political domination of the rural development agenda by agribusiness has thrived at the expense of the interests of farmworkers, small family farms, rural communities, the general public, wildlife, and the environment.

[...]

"Fighting fire with fire will only result in a conflagration—farmers deserve solutions that will not fail in a few years, and land them in an even deeper hole."

Superweeds Make Evident the Need for Sustainable Solutions

Union of Concerned Scientists

In the following viewpoint, the Union of Concerned Scientists (UCS) bring attention to the issue of superweeds caused by farming with seeds genetically engineered to be resistant to herbicides. Promoting farming practices based on agroecology, the UCS argues for public policies that incentivize farmers to utilize healthy practices with long-term benefits. The UCS is a non-profit science advocacy group founded in 1969 by scientists and students at the Massachusetts Institute of Technology (MIT). The UCS's goal is to develop scientific research and innovation to solve the world's pressing environmental and social problems.

"'Superweeds' Resulting from Monsanto's Products Overrun US Farm Landscape," Union of Concerned Scientists (www.ucsusa.org), December 11, 2013. Reprinted by permission.

As you read, consider the following questions:

1. According to the viewpoint, what problems are "superweeds" causing across the United States?
2. According to the viewpoint, what are the causes for overall herbicide use being significantly higher than before the use of Roundup Ready crops?
3. According to the viewpoint, what practices could reduce herbicide use by more than 90 percent without a loss in farmers' profits?

A plague of out-of-control weeds is cropping up in farm fields across the country. According to a policy brief from the Union of Concerned Scientists (UCS), this epidemic of "superweeds"— weeds that have developed resistance to a common herbicide that once kept them in check—now affects more than 60 million acres of US cropland, wreaking environmental havoc, increasing farmers' costs, and promoting the use of more toxic herbicides.

The brief, "The Rise of Superweeds—and What to Do About It," analyses the problem with existing and proposed technology fixes, and lays out more sustainable ways to control resistant weeds. These alternatives often have multiple benefits for farmers and the public, and need more emphasis from policy makers and the research community.

"It sounds like a bad sci-fi movie or something out of *The Twilight Zone*. But 'superweeds' are real and they're infesting America's croplands," said Doug Gurian-Shermand, senior scientist with the UCS Food & Environment Program and author of the paper. "Overuse of Monsanto's 'Roundup Ready' seeds and herbicides in our industrial farming system is largely to blame. And if we're not careful, the industry's proposed 'solutions' could make this epidemic much worse."

When Monsanto's "Roundup Ready" product line went on the market 17 years ago, it was supposed to reduce herbicide use. This convenient system of engineered seeds designed to work with the company's Roundup herbicide enabled farmers to apply herbicides after crops were growing to kill weeds while leaving their crops unharmed. Farmers enthusiastically adopted these products as they saved time and made weed control easier. And initially, overall herbicide use declined.

The benefits were short lived. Weed species began evolving resistance to glyphosate, the active ingredient in Roundup, in the United States within five years. Fifty percent of US farmers surveyed report glyphosate-resistant weed infestations. In the Southeast, more than 90 percent of cotton and soybean farmers are affected. Today, 24 species of weeds have developed resistance, and as a result, overall herbicide use is far higher than before Roundup Ready crops. If the Roundup Ready crops had never been planted, it is estimated farmers would have eliminated 404 million pounds of pesticides.

The US's outdated farming system is also part of the problem. For years, farming policies have encouraged farmers to plant the same crop year after year. This system, called monoculture, provides a superb breeding ground for weeds, and has accelerated the development of resistance.

Some resistant weeds can grow eight feet tall and the tough stems damage farm equipment. Removing them by hand can be the only option, and an expensive one. These weeds steal nutrients from the crops, which reduces yields, overall productivity, and farmers' profits.

"Monsanto and other agribusiness companies are now touting herbicide-resistant crops engineered to withstand older, more toxic herbicides, such as dicamba and 2,4-D, as the 'solution.' These new herbicides will certainly exacerbate the problem, but increase the companies' bottom lines," said Gurian-Sherman. "It's a highly risky move. Increased herbicides use on the new engineered crops will speed up weed resistance, leaving no viable herbicide alternatives. This is a dangerous chemical cocktail, that when combined with the current farming system, it's a recipe for disaster."

In fact, these next generation herbicide-tolerant crops are likely to speed up the development of weeds that are resistant to multiple herbicides. If weeds resistant to glyphosate become resistant to dicamba or 2,4-D, and several other major herbicides, there would be no other good alternative herbicides to fight what would be the ultimate superweeds. There are no silver bullet herbicides in the chemical pipeline to bail farmers out when current herbicides fail.

Moreover, dicamba and 2,4-D pose additional risks to people and nearby crops. These herbicides have been linked to increased rates of certain diseases, including non-Hodgkin's lymphoma, in farmers and farm workers. They are prone to drifting on the wind and dispersing into the air after application, and consequently, the herbicides can settle far from where they were applied. These herbicides are extremely toxic to many of the most common fruit and vegetable crops, as well as to plants that provide food and habitat for pollinators and other beneficial insects.

There is a better way to help farmers combat superweeds, through public policies that provide incentives for "healthy farming" practices based on the science of agroecology. These practices include rotating crops and planting cover crops. If implemented, such practices could reduce herbicides use by more than 90 percent, while keeping weeds in check and even increasing farmers' profits.

UCS recommends increased funding for the USDA's Conservation Stewardship Program, which offers financial incentives for farmers using sustainable weed control methods. More resources should also be directed toward multidisciplinary research on integrated weed management strategies, and technical assistance to help farmers adopt them. The new generation of herbicide resistant crops should not be approved without adequate safeguards to protect the public and reduce the possibility of more resistant weeds.

"Fighting fire with fire will only result in a conflagration— farmers deserve solutions that will not fail in a few years, and land them in an even deeper hole," said Gurian-Sherman. "Instead of favoring the same industrial methods and genetically engineered products that got farmers into this mess, public policies should promote healthy farming practices that can produce long-term benefits for American farmers, consumers, and the natural resources we all depend upon."

> *"Who has made money from GM technology? Seed and chemical companies. Big farmers, too. Little farmers have gained less, and have had to trade away more privileges."*

Chemical Corporations Are the Main Beneficiaries of GMOs

Nathanael Johnson

In the following viewpoint, Nathanael Johnson investigates how the profits from GMOs are dispersed and who stands to benefit the most. Johnson establishes that although consumers are not entirely without benefits, GM technology is largely a product for the profit of the chemical companies who produce GM seeds and the big farmers who buy from them. Johnson is a journalist and senior food writer for Grist. *He has taught in the Graduate School of Journalism at the University of California, Berkeley, and written two books.*

As you read, consider the following questions:

1. How are farmers able to profit from buying GM seeds if they are more expensive than non-GM seeds?
2. What benefits do consumers gain from GMOs?
3. What tradeoff do small farmers make when using GM seeds?

"Golden Apple or Forbidden Fruit? Following the Money on GMOs," by Nathanael Johnson, Grist Magazine, Inc., September 16, 2013. Reprinted by permission.

Much of the battle over transgenic crops has occurred in the realm of science fiction. There, entirely hypothetical health risks square off against visions of wondrous but imaginary benefits. This isn't nearly as ridiculous as it sounds: To decide which technologies to pursue and which to avoid, modern Jules Vernes need to dream up best and worst-case scenarios.

The problem is, the debate tends to get stuck in the future. We've had transgenic plants for nearly two decades, which is enough time to fairly ask, who has actually benefited from genetically modified crops? We've had these plants long enough now that we don't have to look to fantastic visions of the future; we can simply look at the reality.

In search of reality, I began emailing economists, lawyers, and advocates to ask them this question. The first to answer was Andrew Kimbrell, executive director of the Center for Food Safety. Kimbrell said the companies that bet on GM technology have been its greatest beneficiaries. "The chemical companies, right? The big five: Monsanto, DuPont, Dow, Bayer, and Syngenta … No. 2 would be farmers, specifically big farmers, because it makes their herbicide application a lot easier."

Farmers pay more to buy the GM seed, and more for the herbicides to treat herbicide-resistant crops, but they save on labor costs. Rather than meticulously spritzing individual weeds by hand to avoid killing the crop, farmers can quickly spray an entire field when using herbicide-resistant plants, Kimbrell said.

Beneficiary No. 3? There is none, according to Kimbrell. "These companies have completely failed, in over 30 years, to come up with a trait that benefits a consumer. Nobody gets up in the morning wanting to buy a genetically engineered food."

I could think of exceptions: Papaya genetically engineered to resist ringspot virus is more appealing to many consumers than diseased fruit. But these are exceptions that prove the rule; the vast majority of transgenic plants are designed to make farmers, rather than eaters, happy.

What about price? I asked Kimbrell. Do we eaters see lower prices because of genetic modification?

"No. There are no lower prices. GMOs have not lowered prices at all. They have massively increased prices for seed."

Indeed, seed prices bumped up with the introduction of genetically modified varieties.

What about GM crops lifting small farmers out of poverty? Kimbrell scoffed at that. "Smallholders can't afford to buy [the herbicides] RoundUp and 2,4-D," he said.

Ask people on opposite sides of this issue if genetic modification benefits the poor and you'll hear wildly different claims. Kimbrell's point is that GM crops are designed to save farmers time and money if they are involved in high-tech agriculture. Vandana Shiva, an environmental activist and longtime critic of industrial agriculture, has pointed to cases in which small farmers in India have killed themselves when the debt they've taken on to buy seed, fertilizer, and pesticides grows too crushing.

On the other hand, biotech industry consultant Clive James maintains that GM crops are a ladder to prosperity. James has calculated that in 2012, for the first time, farmers in the developing world planted more GM seed than farmers in industrialized nations. These farmers must have a reason for seeking out transgenics.

As usual in this debate, I find myself stranded between irreconcilable claims. But fortunately, it turns out there's a large body of economic analyses that have asked precisely the same question I have: Who has benefited?

One of the people I'd emailed, UC Berkeley agricultural economist David Zilberman, sent me a short note from the Ivory Coast suggesting that the benefits of GE food are widespread:

"The seed companies captured less than 50 percent of the economic gains in most studies (frequently less than 30 percent)," he wrote. "The rest [is] distributed between farmers and consumers."

The studies Zilberman consulted on this question have found that the biotech industry captures between 10 and 70 percent of the money generated by their transgenic seeds. The rest of the benefit (30 to 90 percent) is shared by US farmers, US eaters, and the rest of the world. That's a huge range, but it's interesting that every study examining this issue has found that consumers do benefit from food prices. It may not be much—less than 2 percent is the estimate at the lower end—but the average Joe and Jane are probably getting some extra change thanks to GMOs.

OK. Now, what do the economists say about small farmers? Are GM crops lifting them out of poverty or driving them to suicide? A review of the economic publications on this question found that:

> During the first decade of their use by smallholder farmers in developing economies, peer-reviewed research has indicated that, on average, transgenic crops do provide economic advantages for adopting farmers.

But hold on: That average hides all sorts of highs and lows. I love this review, done by the International Food Policy Research Institute, because the authors carefully noted the problems with each analysis. For instance one study, following the introduction of GM cotton to the Makhathini Flats in South Africa, found that small farmers were major beneficiaries of the technology. But another, more thorough, analysis suggested something more complex: Small farmers had made a little more money with the transgenic cotton, but only because the Vunisa Cotton company had set them up for success.

Vunisa pitched the transgenic seed to farmers; supplied them with pesticides, fertilizer, loans, and advisors; and then bought up all their cotton. Farmers are vulnerable when they can only buy from, and sell to, one company. That company can ratchet up the cost of seed, while ratcheting down the amount it pays for cotton. So in the Makhathini Flats, farmers were making a little more money—at least for the first few years—but they were also in a much more precarious position.

And this example is part of a theme. In general, GM crops do seem to give small farmers an economic boost, but the studies rarely look at the bigger political and economic tradeoffs those farmers are making. Those tradeoffs do sometimes have dire consequences—like farmer suicide.

But it doesn't look like the introduction of GM crops is responsible for a large percentage of those deaths. The sad fact is that a lot of farmers kill themselves in India. The numbers didn't budge significantly with the introduction of GM plants. There are, however, many well-documented cases in which debt—in part from the purchase of GM seeds—drove farmers to suicide. That's absolutely true. It's more accurate to say that suicides are caused by the bigger economic monster: The system that requires farmers to take on extravagant debt to compete.

A small farmer who owns his land and saves his seeds each year is relatively independent. A farmer who must take out loans to buy GM seeds, fertilizer, irrigation equipment, and pesticides is beholden and making a riskier (though also potentially more lucrative) bet. For each technological innovation, farmers trade some of their independence for a shot at greater profit. Perhaps it's fair to say GM seeds are a synecdoche—a part that represents the whole—for the larger system that's causing farmer suicide in India, especially in those areas where the only seed available to farmers is genetically modified.

So who has made money from GM technology? Seed and chemical companies, for sure. Big farmers, too. Little farmers have gained less, and have had to trade away more privileges. And the rest of us probably pay a little less for GMO food (industrial meat, for example). And all of this is a little fuzzy, because economics is an inexact science, and the studies are still coming in.

The question of who benefits goes beyond money, of course. We also need to look at the environment: Some see GM crops as an environmental savior, while other say they are a disaster. I'm going to make my usual kamikaze run into this minefield to see if there's any way to reconcile the evidence each side presents.

Before I do that, though, I'm going to talk to some farmers and learn what the pluses and minuses look like from their perspective. Do farmers feel they are trading away intangibles for each new technological advancement?

> *"Crop protection chemicals have an important contribution to make to the global challenge of producing more food from the same area of farming land."*

Using Pesticides Produces Greater Crop Yields

Sarah Armstrong and John Clough

In the following viewpoint Sarah Armstrong and John Clough argue that crop protection chemicals allow for significantly greater crop yields and are a vital part of the solution to global food shortages. Although there have been problems with past chemicals, the authors claim that modern products are more refined, making them safer for both consumers and the environment. Armstrong and Clough are research chemists who work for Syngenta, a global biotechnology company that produces agrochemicals and seeds.

As you read, consider the following questions:

1. What percentages of greater crop yields does the viewpoint cite in favor of the benefits of crop protection chemicals?
2. How does crop loss impact consumers?
3. How are natural products important to the crop protection industry?

About 800 chemicals are registered for use in crop protection around the world, representing a major multi-billion-dollar industry. Several global companies make it their business to discover, develop and sell new products, one of which can cost the company ca $200m to bring to the market. A typical research programme may take five years, and this is followed by a development period of around eight years, during which time the chemical will be rigorously tested to ensure that it meets the highest standards of safety—to farmers, consumers and in the environment. In addition, the route by which the compound will be prepared on a multi-tonne scale is determined during this development period. But are these chemicals the answer to food sustainability and what is the outlook for the development of new products?

The Benefits of Crop Protection Chemicals

Crop protection chemicals provide farmers with a cost-effective way of improving the yield and the quality of their crops. They also make harvesting more straightforward and maintain consistent yields from year to year.

The main classes of crop protection chemicals are herbicides, insecticides and fungicides. Selective herbicides, for example, control the growth of weeds which would otherwise grow among a crop, competing with it for water, nutrients and sunlight. Without crop protection chemicals agriculture would be less efficient.

Research done over the past 20 years, mainly by Dr Erich-Christian Oerke and his colleagues at the University of Bonn in Germany, has shown that overall crop yields would be around half their current levels without the use of crop protection products. In certain crops, for example cotton, which can be spoilt by a host of different insects and competing weeds, the losses can be as high as 80 per cent.

Research has also been done by other groups to compare yields obtained from crops grown organically, where the use of crop protection products is minimised. (Generally no synthetic crop protection chemicals are used, though minerals, such as copper salts, and natural chemicals, such as the insecticide rotenone found in the roots of several plants, may be.) The findings suggest that organic yields are usually well below those achieved when crop protection chemicals are used, typically 30 per cent lower for wheat and barley, and 40 per cent lower for potatoes.

Moreover entire crops have been lost without the use of crop protection chemicals. Potatoes and vines are examples of particularly high-risk crops, growing in parts of the world where weather conditions can at times be conducive to fungal epidemics. The devastation of entire crops is of major concern, both to farmers, who lose income, and to consumers, who face rising supermarket prices.

Modern Crop Protection Chemicals

Inorganic compounds, such as arsenic and mercury salts, were used in agriculture until the 19th century to control insects and fungi, respectively. These practices continued until the 1930s, when simple synthetic organic chemicals, eg the herbicide 2,4-D (dichlorophenoxy ethanoic acid) and the insecticide DDT (dichlorodiphenyltrichloroethane) came on the market.

Crop protection chemistry has come a long way since then. Modern products are designed to be highly selective in their action to minimise the impact on non-target organisms. Selective activity enables, for example, the control of fungi growing on plants without damaging the plants themselves; or the control of a range of weed species without damaging the crop plants among which the weeds are growing. An essential aspect of the selectivity of a crop protection chemical is that it does not affect the consumer or the environment. Each of these effects may stem from specificity at the enzyme or receptor level, or from selective metabolism.

There has also been a trend towards the use of lower application rates for these chemicals, though this can really only be seen by looking back over decades rather than years. For example, the herbicide 2,4-D is typically applied at rates of about 1000g ha-1, while the best of the modern herbicides such as the sulfonylureas are effective at rates as low as 10g ha-1.

Modern compounds are also safer than their older counterparts, and the hurdles for registration are higher than in the past. Residual levels in food are measured to ensure they do not pose a health risk, and their persistence in the environment and bioaccumulation are also determined.

Herbicides

The non-selective herbicide glyphosate was introduced by Monsanto in 1973. This herbicide controls the growth of a wide variety of plants, both weeds and crops, and compounds of this type can be used as an alternative to ploughing. Glyphosate was discovered during a chemistry-led research programme in which more than 100 novel aminomethylphosphonic acids were synthesised and tested for interesting properties in a variety of screens. Farmers use glyphosate when they want to clear all the plants from a field. The herbicide kills even perennial plants, since it can move from the leaf, where the spray droplets fall, into the root.

Glyphosate inhibits 5-enolpyruvylshikimate-3-phosphate synthase (EPSPS), an enzyme involved in the biosynthesis of aromatic amino acids, which are required for protein biosynthesis and thus plant growth. This enzyme is absent in mammals (which rely on plants in their diet for aromatic amino acids), so glyphosate has little toxicity. The compound is also safe in the environment, since it binds to soil and degrades quickly.

Mesotrione, a Syngenta product, is one of a family of herbicides which inhibit 4-hydroxyphenylpyruvate dioxygenase (HPPD), an enzyme on the biochemical pathway that leads to plastoquinone, a co-factor in carotenoid biosynthesis. (Carotenoids are essential pigments in plants which harvest light energy for growth and protect the plant from photodamage.) Mesotrione is a selective herbicide, providing post-emergence control of broad-leaf weeds in maize, and is often used in mixtures with other herbicides to take advantage of dual modes of action.

Mesosulfuron-methyl was developed by chemists at Bayer CropScience and is a member of the sulfonylurea family of herbicides that act by inhibiting the enzyme acetolactate synthase (ALS), which catalyses a step in the biosynthesis of branched-chain amino acids. It is used for the post-emergence control of grasses and some broad-leaf weeds in cereal crops at rates as low as 15g ha-1.

Fungicides

Azoxystrobin, the world's largest-selling fungicide, was discovered and developed by Syngenta chemists. A broad-spectrum member of the strobilurin family, this fungicide acts by inhibiting mitochondrial respiration in fungi by binding at a specific site on cytochrome b, and thereby blocking the production of adenosine triphosphate (ATP) and suppressing the energy cycle.

The azoles, compounds containing a 1,2,4-triazole (or, in a few cases, an imidazole) ring, are another important class of fungicide. They act by inhibiting the biosynthesis of ergosterol, an important component of fungal cell walls. Epoxiconazole, developed by BASF, is one of the leading compounds of this class. It has a broad spectrum of preventative and curative activity and is used, for example, in cereals, sugar beet, peanuts and oilseed rape.

Mandipropamid, a mandelic acid amide fungicide, was launched by Syngenta in 2007. It is used to prevent damage caused by various fungal diseases such as downy mildew on grapes and late blight on potatoes.

Insecticides

The pyrethroids are a major class of insecticides, and have been in use for over 25 years. Their synthesis was inspired by the natural pyrethrins. λ-Cyhalothrin is used for the control of insects in a range of crops, including cereals, cotton and potatoes, and works by disrupting the central nervous system of insects. The chemical interferes with the function of membrane-spanning sodium channels, leading ultimately to paralysis and death.

Thiamethoxam (Syngenta) is an insecticide of the neonicotinoid family, first sold in 1997, and used to control aphids, whiteflies, thrips, hoppers and other insect pests in a wide variety of crops, including rice, soybean, cereals, sugar beet and cotton. Again, it interferes with the nervous system of insects but, in this case, is an agonist of the nicotinic acetylcholine receptor.

Rynaxypyr, a new insecticide from DuPont, has recently received approval for use in the US and Canada. It selectively blocks calcium ion channels crucial for muscle function in insects. It will be used in a variety of fruit and vegetable crops, including apples, grapes, tomatoes and lettuce.

Growing Resistance

Despite the availability of so many chemicals for crop protection, there is always scope to replace some of the older products with better ones, especially those where resistance is becoming a problem.

The onset of resistance, though difficult to predict, is a feature of modern compounds with a specific biochemical mode of action. Small changes in the target organism, at the target site for example, render the compounds ineffective.

The broad-spectrum herbicide glyphosate is the world's largest-selling crop protection chemical. It is used in partnership with maize and soya which have been genetically engineered to be resistant to its effects. However, after many years of extensive use, in 1996, several species of glyphosate-resistant weeds emerged, followed by others from many parts of the world. So glyphosate will ultimately need a replacement and the discovery of such a compound will be a glittering prize for any crop protection company.

Another driver for the search for new and improved products are the re-registration programmes currently going on in various regions of the world, including Europe. These programmes are aimed at ensuring that all crop protection chemicals meet modern safety and environmental standards. The re-registration procedure is expensive, and the cost has to be met by the manufacturers. As a consequence, some of the smaller products are being lost to the farmer because their sales don't justify the costs associated with re-registration.

In Search of New Crop Protection Chemicals

Chemists often work for long periods, sometimes years, in their search for new products, without discovering the one compound they are looking for that meets all of the following criteria:

- high potency against a suitable spectrum of weeds, insects or fungi;

- high selectivity, allowing the compound to be applied at low rates and without affecting non-target organisms;

- chemical and metabolic stability, so that it survives in sunlight on the surface of a leaf, and then during translocation to its biochemical target within the plant, but without being so stable that it persists in the environment.

As a consequence, successful projects have to lead to highly profitable new products which pay not only for themselves but also for all the unsuccessful research.

The research involves the synthesis and biological screening of many compounds. However, new technologies, especially advances in robotics, automation and data-handling, have dramatically changed the way in which a research project is done. For example, preliminary screens have been miniaturised, and test chemicals can now be applied to plants, fungi and insects growing in 96-well microtitre plates. The plates are bar-coded and handled robotically, and the test chemicals, now required only in milligram quantities, are sprayed into the wells by computer-controlled instruments.

Chemists are also able to use automation to make sets of related compounds in parallel using the same synthetic steps, sometimes hundreds at a time, by "combinatorial chemistry" or "parallel synthesis." In fact, it is not difficult to make large numbers of compounds, the real skill is to design sets of compounds with diverse structures, and properties which are likely to lead to biological activity. Combinatorial chemistry has not been greatly successful as a way to generate new leads, but it is used to make targeted sets of chemicals more efficiently during optimisation programmes.

Nature is a rich source of biologically active compounds. Many plants, for example, produce insecticides to protect themselves, and micro-organisms are also prolific producers of bioactive natural products. Natural products are important to the crop protection industry because they often have novel structures and modes of action. However, they do not usually have the properties required for a crop protection chemical. Poor photostability, for example, is sometimes a problem. Instead, they serve as inspiration for programmes of synthesis, which lead to structurally related compounds, tailored to the properties required by a crop protection chemical.

Finally, every company carefully monitors its competitors' patents to identify new areas of interest, looking for loopholes that can be exploited. Although this approach is probably the most reliable way to find biological activity, it is not without its problems. By definition, the competitor is ahead of the game and, before long, several companies are likely to be working on closely-related chemistry and racing each other to the patent office.

Outlook

The world has recently had a wake-up call over food shortages, and climate change will also present agriculture with future challenges. People now realise how precarious the balance is between supply and demand. Crop protection chemicals have an important contribution to make to the global challenge of producing more food from the same area of farming land.

| *"If the prime purpose of a food system is to nourish people and keep them healthy, this one is failing."*

Agrochemical Farming Is Harmful and Will Not Achieve Food Security

Felicity Lawrence

In the following viewpoint, Felicity Lawrence argues that the increasingly aggressive model of agrochemical farming is not as successful as its proponents claim, and that in the long-term, it actually produces less than diverse ecological farming. Claiming that food production is stuck in a harmful and ineffective rut, Lawrence pushes for change in the way food security for the world is achieved. Lawrence is a special correspondent on the politics of food for The Guardian *and the author of two books on the food industry.*

As you read, consider the following questions:

1. What factors have prompted the recent mergers of the global agrochemical companies?
2. What are the long-term shortcomings of the intensive model of agriculture?
3. How has Flamingo Homegrown reinvented its approach to agriculture to be more ecological?

"Agrichemicals and Ever More Intensive Farming Will Not Feed the World," by Felicity Lawrence, Guardian News and Media Limited, October 2, 2016. Reprinted by permission.

B ritish farmers growing wheat typically treat each crop over its growing cycle with four fungicides, three herbicides, one insecticide and one chemical to control molluscs. They buy seed that has been precoated with chemicals against insects. They spray the land with weedkiller before planting, and again after.

They apply chemical growth regulators that change the balance of plant hormones to control the height and strength of the grain's stem. They spray against aphids and mildew. And then they often spray again just before harvesting with the herbicide glyphosate to desiccate the crop, which saves them the energy costs of mechanical drying.

Most farmers around the world, whatever the crop, will turn to one of just six companies that dominate the market to buy all these agrochemicals and their seeds. The concentration of power over primary agriculture in such a small number of corporations, and their ability both to set prices and determine the varieties available, has already been a cause of concern among farmers. Yet by next year the competition is likely to shrink even further.

The six global chemical and seed giants will become three behemoths with even greater market control. Just when climate change demands a more diverse and adaptable food system, resilient to changing conditions, agriculture is being dragged further down an ever-narrowing agroindustrial route.

Bayer, Monsanto, Dupont, Dow, Syngenta and BASF currently account for three-quarters of the global agrochemical market and nearly two-thirds of the commercial seed market. As commodity prices have fallen, their profits have been flagging. Farmers who are getting less for their crops have struggled to make money. In the US they have begun turning away from expensive GM seed, and in Europe more than 3m farms have been lost in eight years. So for two years the agrochemical companies have been engaged in a flurry of merger and acquisition activity to become even bigger and more powerful. The bids have settled, for the moment, on a trio of megadeals.

The most recently agreed merger, worth $66bn, is between Monsanto, the controversial US-headquartered giant that is the world's largest seed and seventh-largest pesticide company, and

German-based Bayer, the world's second-largest agrochemical and seventh-largest seed company.

To give a sense of the scale of this deal and its impact, Monsanto, as well as being the leading global supplier of genetically modified seed, controls nearly a quarter of the vegetable seed market in Europe and is a big player in conventional maize seed. The herbicide glyphosate, its big earner, is now so commonly used across Europe that it has been detected in the urine of 44% of people surveyed for Friends of the Earth. Bayer is a leader in most pesticides, including neonicotinoids used to treat about 90% of UK cereal, sugar beet and oil seed rape.

The proposed Bayer-Monsanto merger follows a $130bn deal between the US corporates DuPont (No 2 in seeds, 6 in pesticides) and the Dow Chemical company (5 in seeds, 4 in pesticides). China, focused on its own food security, wants a bit of the action too, and its state-backed agrochemical company ChemChina (seventh in global pesticide sales via subsidiaries) has successfully bid $43bn for Swiss Syngenta. A parallel process of concentration is taking place in the fertiliser sector.

The narrative offered to justify this dominance of a supposedly free market is that only bigger, braver new entities can rise to the great challenge of our time: how to feed an additional 3 billion people by 2050 without destroying the planet. We are asked to accept the intensive model of agriculture as the heroic march of science, against primitive, low-yielding, traditional methods of production. There is no alternative. But in fact it is this model of food production that is stuck in a rut.

Postwar, there were indeed huge strides in increasing the amount of food produced globally thanks to plant breeding and the use of chemicals in the form of artificial fertilisers and pesticides. But alongside the triumphs of that green revolution, its longer-term shortcomings are increasingly apparent.

Overuse of agrochemicals has contributed to steep losses in biodiversity, and crucially of pollinators vital to food. Increases in pest resistance threaten to reverse previous gains in yields. Research has found that over a short period yields per hectare for individual crops are greater in intense agricultural systems. But over a longer period, and when you look at total farm output, more mixed and diverse farming produces more.

If the prime purpose of a food system is to nourish people and keep them healthy, this one is failing. Despite a doubling of available food in some regions, more than 750 million people still routinely go hungry. At the same time nearly 2 billion are overweight or obese.

The agroindustrial system these companies underpin is primarily focused on a small number of commodity crops for export. The ETC research group points out that GM seed companies have concentrated their development efforts on maize, soya and rapeseed (canola) rather than a wide range of the 7,000-odd food crops grown by farmers around the world. Breaking these commodity crops down into their constituent parts and reselling them as sugars, starches, and fats adds shareholder value in the chain but depletes nutritional value. Diet-related diseases have now overtaken infectious diseases as the largest cause of premature death globally.

Although the companies talk of tackling the threat that climate change poses to food security, the agroindustrial food system is one of the most significant causes of it, contributing a third of all manmade greenhouse gas emissions.

Corporate concentration in the food system has sucked the money to be made in the chain up to a handful of companies at the top. It works for the few but not for the many. As if to underline the point, the chief executive of Monsanto stands to collect over $135m from the Bayer merger in share options and severance pay. But paradoxically, these three mergers to increase power reveal a sector that is also vulnerable. The pesticide business is under pressure—Bayer and Syngenta are both big producers of the three types of neonicotinoids recently banned in the EU because of their impact on bees. The EU has been under pressure too to restrict the use of glyphosate, since it was ruled a "probable carcinogen" by the WHO last year.

This way of producing our food is broken and most people, including those still promoting it, know it. So why does it not change?

The former UN rapporteur on the right to food, Olivier de Schutter, has described a series of "lock-ins" that prevent change. Because value accrues to a limited number of actors, their political and economic power and ability to influence government policy is reinforced.

The latest frontier is Africa, where there is a new scramble to spread the agroindustrial model of farming. It may well be in Africa, however, that a different, more ecological vision of the food future emerges. I had a glimmer of it on a trip to a large-scale horticultural export company based on Kenya's Lake Naivasha.

The company, Flamingo Homegrown, has abandoned its long and heavy use of chemical pesticides, partly in response to a campaign highlighting their effect on workers' health, but partly too in recognition that they were on a losing treadmill of spraying and pest resistance.

They have reinvented their agriculture in a way that makes the science of agrochemical use look as primitive as a blunderbuss. Instead they employ groups of highly trained African scientists to study and reproduce in labs the fungi and microrrhizae in healthy soil that form intricate links with plant roots. Rather than waging chemical war on the land, they are working to harness its immensely complex ecosystems. They have built vast greenhouses dedicated to breeding and harvesting ladybirds to control pests biologically rather than chemically.

There is an another route to food security—and it is the polar opposite of three agrochemical giants bestriding the world.

Periodical and Internet Sources Bibliography

The following articles have been selected to supplement the diverse views presented in this chapter.

Gerald Baron, "What You Think about Pesticides Dependson Your Farm Literacy," *Crosscut,* March 13, 2018. https://crosscut. com/2018/03/what-you-think-about-pesticides-depends-your-farm-literacy

Christ D'Angelo, "GMOs Ruled Safe to Eat, But They Aren't Solving World Hunger," *The Huffington Post,* May 18, 2016. https://www.huffingtonpost.com/entry/gmo-report-safe-to-eat_us_573bac3fe4b0646cbeeb61b6

Hannah Devlin, "Plants Modified to Boost Photosynthesis Produce Greater Yields, Study Shows," *The Guardian,* November 17, 2016. https://www.theguardian.com/science/2016/nov/17/plants-genetically-modified-to-boost-photosynthesis-produce-greater-yields-study-shows

Caitlin Dewey, "'Miracle' Weed Killer That Was Supposed to Save Farms Is Killing Them Instead," *The Independent,* August 30, 2017. https://www.independent.co.uk/news/world/americas/miracle-weed-killer-poisoning-crops-farms-agriculture-herbicide-arkansas-a7919861.html

Jocelyn Gecker, "California Bans Use of Some Farming Pesticides Near Schools," *The Seattle Times,* November 7, 2017. https://www.seattletimes.com/nation-world/california-bans-some-pesticides-near-schools/

Danny Hakim, "Doubts about the Promised Bounty of Genetically Modified Crops," *New York Times,* October 29, 2016. https://www.nytimes.com/2016/10/30/business/gmo-promise-falls-short.html?rref=collection%2Ftimestopic%2FGenetically%20Modified%20Food

Caroline Newman, "Largest-Ever Study Reveals Environmental Impact of Genetically Modified Crops," UVA Today, September 14, 2016. https://news.virginia.edu/content/largest-ever-study-reveals-environmental-impact-genetically-modified-crops

OPPOSING
VIEWPOINTS®
SERIES

Chapter 3

Do GMOs Pose a Threat to Our Health?

Chapter Preface

G enetically modified organisms, more commonly abbreviated as GMOs, are perhaps the most divisive matter of scientific controversy today. According to a 2015 poll by Pew Research Center, a nonpartisan fact tank that seeks to inform the public about the issues and attitudes shaping the world, only 37 percent of the general public believe genetically modified food to be safe, in comparison to 88 percent of scientists. This is a gap in belief greater than on any other contentious issues such as evolution, vaccinations, and climate change, and the public's opinion has stayed relatively consistent despite the efforts of pro-GMO groups to present their case in various ways.

Proponents of GM foods have often asserted that millions of people have been consuming GMOs for the past 20 years without any signs of adverse effects, and that numerous safety tests have been conducted. In response, GMO opponents have argued that a lack of issues thus far does not necessarily signify that GM foods are completely safe and that the possibility exists for long-term health effects that we simply don't yet know of. Multiple studies have come out on the safety of GMO products, some even contending that they are more beneficial to our health than non-GMO crops due to reduced toxins and increased nutritional value, but these reports have been criticized for lack of reliable evidence, unsatisfactory tests often conducted over short periods of time, and the overstatement of scientific endorsements of safety.

With both sides having legitimate claims to support their case and justifiable concerns that cannot always be assuaged through the currently available empirical data, the nuanced debate has been going back and forth for years and shows no signs of reaching a reconciliation.

The following chapter examines claims on the safety of GMOs, focusing on the issue of whether there is or is not a scientific consensus on their safety and the differences between gene-editing and conventional plant breeding.

> "So let's be clear once again: the safety debate is over. If you vaccinate your kids and believe that climate change is real, you need to stop being scared of genetically modified foods."

Scientific Consensus on GMOs Say They're Safe

Mark Lynas

In the following viewpoint, Mark Lynas argues that GMOs are unequivocally safe and that continual debate over the issue is unproductive and worrisome. He asserts that anti-GMO environmental groups demonize GMOs to the extent of science denialism and states that the percentage of the public that believes GE foods are safe as compared to scientists is a greater gap than any other issue of scientific controversy. Lynas is the author of several books on the environment and a visiting fellow at Cornell University's Office of International Programs at the College of Agriculture and Life Sciences. He also works with the Cornell Alliance for Science.

"GMO Safety Debate Is Over," by Mark Lynas, Cornell Alliance for Science, May 23, 2016. Reprinted by permission.

As you read, consider the following questions:

1. According to the viewpoint, did the National Academies report find any links between GMOs and health issues?
2. According to the viewpoint, what are some reasons as to why attitudes toward GMOs are resistant to change?
3. According to the viewpoint, what are the areas for genuine debate over GMOs?

The GMO debate is over again. Last week, the prestigious National Academies of Science, Engineering and Medicine issued what is probably the most far-reaching report ever produced by the scientific community on genetically engineered food and crops. The conclusion was unambiguous: Having examined hundreds of scientific papers written on the subject, sat through hours of live testimony from activists and considered hundreds more comments from the general public, the scientists wrote that they "found no substantiated evidence that foods from GE crops were less safe than foods from non-GE crops."

The National Academies process was both impressively inclusive and explicitly consensual. As noted in the preface to their report, the scientists "took all of the comments" however ludicrous "as constructive challenges" and considered them carefully. Thus the expert committee patiently gave yogic flyer-turned-anti-GMO activist Jeffrey Smith a generous 20-minute slot within which to make his customary assertion that genetically engineered foods cause just about every imaginable modern ailment. Greenpeace also offered invited testimony. So did Giles-Eric Seralini, the French professor who suffered the ultimate scientific indignity of having his paper claiming rats fed GMOs suffered tumors retracted in 2013.

Each of their claims was examined in turn. Do GE foods cause cancer? No patterns of changing cancer incidence over time are "generally similar" between the US, where GMO foods are ubiquitous, and the United Kingdom, where they are virtually unknown. How about kidney disease? US rates have barely budged over a quarter century. Obesity or diabetes? There is "no published evidence to support the hypothesis" of a link between them and GE foods. Celiac disease? "No major difference" between the US and UK again. Allergies? "The committee did not find a relationship between consumption of GE foods and the increase in prevalence of food allergies." Autism? Again, evidence comparing the US and UK "does not support the hypothesis of a link."

In a rational world, everyone previously fearful about the health effects of GMOs would read the report, breathe a huge sigh of relief and start looking for more evidence-based explanations for worrying trends in health issues like diabetes, autism and food allergies. But psychological associations developed over many years are difficult to break. A Pew Center poll in 2015 found only 37 percent of the public thought GE foods were safe, as compared to 88 percent of scientists, a greater gap than on any other issue of scientific controversy, including climate change, evolution and childhood vaccinations. These entrenched attitudes are not about to disappear especially since they are continually reinforced by a vocal and well-funded anti-GMO lobby.

There is also political path dependence. Vermont's GMO labeling law, scheduled to throw US food manufacturers and retailers into chaos when it comes into force on July 1, is predicated on the explicit assumption that GE foods may be unsafe. "There is a lack of consensus regarding the validity of the research and science surrounding the safety of genetically engineered foods," Vermont's Act states in its preamble. Indeed, such foods "potentially pose risks to health [and] safety. Will Vermont's legislature reconsider its Act now that it stands so clearly on the wrong side of a rock—solid scientific consensus? Of course not.

The National Academies report should make particularly uncomfortable reading for the environmental movement, many of whose leading member groups now exhibit all the hallmarks of full-scale science denialism on the issue. A spokeswoman from Friends of the Earth dismissed the report as "deceptive" before she had even read it. The group's website claims that "numerous studies" show GE foods can pose "serious risks" to human health. Another environmentalist group, Food and Water Watch, issued a pre-publication rebuttal that conspiratorially accused the National Academies of having undisclosed links with Monsanto, before reasserting its view that "there is no consensus, and there remains a very vigorous debate among scientists … about the safety and merits of this technology."

But despite these shrill denials, the truth is that there is no more of a debate on the safety of GE crops than on reality of climate change, the scientific consensus on which all these same green groups aggressively defend. And the irony goes deeper: many of the strategies now being employed to demonize GMOs come straight out of the climate denialist playbook. There's the same promotion of false "no consensus" statements by groups of self-appointed experts. Why, more than 300 "scientists and legal experts" signed a "no consensus on GMO safety" statement last year, Greenpeace reminds us. That sounds like a lot, until you compare it with the 30,000 "American scientists" who have supposedly signed a petition claiming that there is "no convincing scientific evidence" linking CO_2 with climate change, which Greenpeace (rightly in my view) ignores.

There's also a worrying trend towards the harassment of bona fide scientists. Just as senior Republicans have shamefully targeted climate experts with politically-motivated subpoenas, so an anti-GMO group called US Right to Know has slapped dozens of geneticists and molecular biologists working at public universities with repeated Freedom of Information Act requests demanding access to thousands of their private emails. In some cases, scientists have as a result of subsequent campaigns received death threats, and had their laboratory and home addresses circulated menacingly on social media.

There is still plenty of room for genuine dissent moreover. The National Academies report is zealous in pointing out some of the experienced difficulties and drawbacks of GMOs. The overuse of GE crops has indeed led to the evolution of resistance, both in weeds and insects, it finds. Also, industry domination of the technology might restrict access of small farmers in poorer countries to improved seeds. And mandatory GMO labelling might well be a good way to raise public trust in a more transparent food system.

But these real areas of debate do not include GMO safety. That issue has now been definitively put to bed. So let's be clear once again: the safety debate is over. If you vaccinate your kids and believe that climate change is real, you need to stop being scared of genetically modified foods.

> *"Decisions on the future of our food and agriculture should not be based on misleading and misrepresentative claims by an internal circle of likeminded stakeholders that a 'scientific consensus' exists on GMO safety."*

There Is No Scientific Consensus on GMOs

Angelika Hilbeck et al.

In the following viewpoint, Angelika Hilbeck et al. argue that it is false to say there is a scientific consensus on GMO safety. The authors object to the idea of a consensus by citing issues such as biased or problematic studies, exaggerated safety endorsement claims from scientific and governmental groups, and the lack of epidemiological studies in human populations. Hilbeck is affiliated with the European Network of Scientists for Social and Environmental Responsibility (ENSSER) and the Swiss Federal Institute of Technology. Many of the other authors are also part of ENSSER and most are affiliated with various universities across the world as well.

"No Scientific Consensus on GMO Safety," by Angelika Hilbeck, Rosa Binimelis, Nicolas Defarge, Ricarda Steinbrecher, András Székács, Fern Wickson, Michael Antoniou, Philip L Bereano, Ethel Ann Clark, Michael Hansen, Eva Novotny, Jack Heinemann, Hartmut Meyer, Vandana Shiva and Brian Wynne, Springer Publishing Company, 2015. https://enveurope.springeropen.com/track/pdf/10.1186/s12302-014-0034-1. Licensed under CC BY 4.0.

As you read, consider the following questions:

1. According to the viewpoint, why is it scientifically impossible to study patterns of GM food consumption in North America?
2. According to the viewpoint, what is concerning about many of the studies that conclude the safety of GM foods?
3. According to the viewpoint, how might funding sources be correlated with scientists' positive or negative attitudes toward the environmental risks of GM crops?

Over recent years, a number of scientific research articles have been published that report disturbing results from genetically modified organism (GMO) feeding experiments with different mammals (e.g. rats,[1] pigs[2]). In addition to the usual fierce responses, these have elicited a concerted effort by genetically modified (GM) seed developers and some scientists, commentators, and journalists to construct claims that there is a "scientific consensus" on GMO safety[3-5] and that the debate on this topic is "over."[6]

These claims led a broader independent community of scientists and researchers to come together as they felt compelled to develop a document that offered a balanced account of the current state of dissent in this field, based on published evidence in the scientific literature, for both the interested public and the wider science community. The statement that was developed was then opened up for endorsement from scientists around the world with relevant expertise and capacities to conclude on the current state of consensus/dissent and debate regarding the published evidence on the safety of GMOs.

This statement clearly demonstrates that the claimed consensus on GMO safety does not exist outside of the above depicted internal circle of stakeholders. The health, environment, and agriculture authorities of most nations recognize publicly that no blanket statement about the safety of all GMOs is possible and that they must be assessed on a "case-by-case" basis. Moreover, the claim that it does exist which continues to be pushed in the above listed circles is misleading and misrepresents or outright ignores the currently available scientific evidence and the broad diversity of scientific opinions among scientists on this issue. The claim further encourages a climate of complacency that could lead to a lack of regulatory and scientific rigour and appropriate caution, potentially endangering the health of humans, animals, and the environment.

Science and society do not proceed on the basis of a constructed consensus, as current knowledge is always open to well-founded challenge and disagreement. We endorse the need for further independent scientific inquiry and informed public discussion on GM product safety.

Some of our objections to the claim of a scientific consensus are listed in the following discussion. The original version endorsed by 300 scientists worldwide can be found at the website of the European Network of Scientists for Social and Environmental Responsibility.[7]

Discussion

1. There Is No Consensus on GM Food Safety

Regarding the safety of GM crops and foods for human and animal health, a comprehensive review of animal feeding studies of GM crops found "An equilibrium in the number [of] research groups suggesting, on the basis of their studies, that a number of varieties of GM products (mainly maize and soybeans) are as safe and nutritious as the respective conventional non-GM plant, and those raising still serious concerns." The review also found that most studies concluding that GM foods were as safe and nutritious as those obtained by conventional breeding were "performed by biotechnology companies or associates, which are also responsible [for] commercializing these GM plants."[8]

A separate review of animal feeding studies that is often cited as showing that GM foods are safe included studies that found significant differences in the GM-fed animals. While the review authors dismissed these findings as not biologically significant[9] the interpretation of these differences is the subject of continuing scientific debate[8,10–12] and no consensus exists on the topic.

Rigorous studies investigating the safety of GM crops and foods would normally involve, inter alia, animal feeding studies in which one group of animals is fed GM food and another group is fed an equivalent non-GM diet. Independent studies of this type are rare, but when such studies have been performed, some have revealed toxic effects or signs of toxicity in the GM-fed animals.[2,8,11–13] The concerns raised by these studies have not been followed up by targeted research that could confirm or refute the initial findings.

The lack of scientific consensus on the safety of GM foods and crops is underlined by the recent research calls of the European Union and the French government to investigate the long-term health impacts of GM food consumption in the light of uncertainties raised by animal feeding studies.[14,15] These official calls imply recognition of the inadequacy of the relevant existing scientific research protocols. They call into question the claim that existing research can be deemed conclusive and the scientific debate on biosafety closed.

2. There Are No Epidemiological Studies Investigating Potential Effects of GM Food Consumption on Human Health

It is often claimed that "trillions of GM meals" have been eaten in the US with no ill effects. However, no epidemiological studies in human populations have been carried out to establish whether there are any health effects associated with GM food consumption. As GM foods and other products are not monitored or labelled after release in North America, a major producer and consumer of GM crops, it is scientifically impossible to trace, let alone study, patterns of consumption and their impacts. Therefore, claims that GM foods are safe for human health based on the experience of North American populations have no scientific basis.

3. Claims That Scientific and Governmental Bodies Endorse GMO Safety Are Exaggerated or Inaccurate

Claims that there is a consensus among scientific and governmental bodies that GM foods are safe, or that they are no more risky than non-GM foods,[16,17] are false. For instance, an expert panel of the Royal Society of Canada issued a report that was highly critical of the regulatory system for GM foods and crops in that country. The report declared that it is "scientifically unjustifiable" to presume that GM foods are safe without rigorous scientific testing and that the "default prediction" for every GM food should be that the introduction of a new gene will cause "unanticipated changes" in the expression of other genes, the pattern of proteins produced, and/or metabolic activities. Possible outcomes of these changes identified in the report included the presence of new or unexpected allergens.[18]

A report by the British Medical Association concluded that with regard to the long-term effects of GM foods on human health and the environment, "many unanswered questions remain" and that "safety concerns cannot, as yet, be dismissed completely on the basis of information currently available." The report called for more research, especially on potential impacts on human health and the environment.[19]

Moreover, the positions taken by other organizations have frequently been highly qualified, acknowledging data gaps and potential risks, as well as potential benefits, of GM technology. For example, a statement by the American Medical Association's Council on Science and Public Health acknowledged "a small potential for adverse events ... due mainly to horizontal gene transfer, allergenicity, and toxicity" and recommended that the current voluntary notification procedure practised in the US prior to market release of GM crops be made mandatory.[20] It should be noted that even a "small potential for adverse events" may turn out to be significant, given the widespread exposure of human and animal populations to GM crops.

A statement by the board of directors of the American Association for the Advancement of Science (AAAS) affirming the safety of GM crops and opposing labelling[21] cannot be assumed to represent the view of AAAS members as a whole and was challenged in an open letter by a group of 21 scientists, including many long-standing members of the AAAS.[22] This episode underlined the lack of consensus among scientists about GMO safety.

4. EU Research Project Does Not Provide Reliable Evidence of GM Food Safety

An EU research project[23] has been cited internationally as providing evidence for GM crop and food safety. However, the report based on this project, "A Decade of EU-Funded GMO Research," presents no data that could provide such evidence from long-term feeding studies in animals.

Indeed, the project was not designed to test the safety of any single GM food but to focus on "the development of safety assessment approaches."[24] Only five published animal feeding studies are referenced in the SAFOTEST section of the report, which is dedicated to GM food safety.[25] None of these studies tested a commercialized GM food; none tested the GM food for long-term effects beyond the subchronic period of 90 days; all found differences in the GM-fed animals, which in some cases were statistically significant; and none concluded on the safety of the GM food tested, let alone on the safety of GM foods in general. Therefore, the EU research project provides no evidence for sweeping claims about the safety of any single GM food or of GM crops in general.

5. List of Several Hundred Studies Does Not Show GM Food Safety

A frequently cited claim published on an Internet website that several hundred studies "document the general safety and nutritional wholesomeness of GM foods and feeds"[26] is misleading. Examination of the studies listed reveals that many do not provide evidence of GM food safety and, in fact, some provide evidence of a lack of safety. For example:

- Many of the studies are not toxicological animal feeding studies of the type that can provide useful information about health effects of GM food consumption. The list includes animal production studies that examine parameters of interest to the food and agriculture industry, such as milk yield and weight gain;[27,28] studies on environmental effects of GM crops; and analytical studies of the composition or genetic makeup of the crop.
- Among the animal feeding studies and reviews of such studies in the list, a substantial number found toxic effects and signs of toxicity in GM-fed animals compared with controls.[29-34] Concerns raised by these studies have not been satisfactorily addressed and the claim that the body of research shows a consensus over the safety of GM crops and foods is false and irresponsible.
- Many of the studies were conducted over short periods compared with the animal's total lifespan and cannot detect long-term health effects.[35,36]

We conclude that these studies, taken as a whole, are misrepresented on the Internet website as they do not "document the general safety and nutritional wholesomeness of GM foods and feeds." Rather, some of the studies give serious cause for concern and should be followed up by more detailed investigations over an extended period of time.

6. There Is No Consensus on the Environmental Risks of GM Crops

Environmental risks posed by GM crops include the effects of insecticidal Bt (a bacterial toxin from *Bacillus thuringiensis* engineered into crops) crops on non-target organisms and the effects of the herbicides used in tandem with herbicide-tolerant GM crops.

As with GM food safety, no scientific consensus exists regarding the environmental risks of GM crops. A review of environmental risk assessment approaches for GM crops identified shortcomings in the procedures used and found "no consensus" globally on the methodologies that should be applied, let alone on standardized testing procedures.[37] Some reviews of the published data on Bt crops have found that they can have adverse effects on non-target and beneficial organisms[38-41] effects that are widely neglected in regulatory assessments and by some scientific commentators. Resistance to Bt toxins has emerged in target pests,[42] and problems with secondary (non-target) pests have been noted, for example, in Bt cotton in China.[43,44]

Herbicide-tolerant GM crops have proved equally controversial. Some reviews and individual studies have associated them with increased herbicide use,[45,46] the rapid spread of herbicide-resistant weeds,[47] and adverse health effects in human and animal populations exposed to Roundup, the herbicide used on the majority of GM crops.[48-50]

As with GM food safety, disagreement among scientists on the environmental risks of GM crops may be correlated with funding sources. A peer-reviewed survey of the views of 62 life scientists on the environmental risks of GM crops found that funding and disciplinary training had a significant effect on attitudes. Scientists with industry funding and/or those trained in molecular biology were very likely to have a positive attitude to GM crops and to hold that they do not represent any unique risks, while publicly-funded scientists working independently of GM crop developer companies and/or those trained in ecology were more likely to hold a "moderately negative" attitude to GM crop safety and to emphasize the uncertainty and ignorance involved. The review authors concluded "The strong effects of training and funding might justify certain institutional changes concerning how we organize science and how we make public decisions when new technologies are to be evaluated."[51]

7. International Agreements Show Widespread Recognition of Risks Posed By GM Foods and Crops

The Cartagena Protocol on Biosafety was negotiated over many years and implemented in 2003. The Cartagena Protocol is an international agreement ratified by 166 governments worldwide that seeks to protect biological diversity from the risks posed by GM technology. It embodies the Precautionary Principle in that it allows signatory states to take precautionary measures to protect themselves against threats of damage from GM crops and foods, even in case of a lack of scientific certainty.[52]

Another international body, the UN's Codex Alimentarius, worked with scientific experts for 7 years to develop international guidelines for the assessment of GM foods and crops because of concerns about the risks they pose. These guidelines were adopted by the Codex Alimentarius Commission, of which over 160 nations are members, including major GM crop producers such as the United States.[53]

The Cartagena Protocol and Codex share a precautionary approach to GM crops and foods, in that they agree that genetic engineering differs from conventional breeding and that safety assessments should be required before GM organisms are used in food or released into the environment.

These agreements would never have been negotiated, and the implementation processes elaborating how such safety assessments should be conducted would not currently be happening, without widespread international recognition of the risks posed by GM crops and foods and the unresolved state of existing scientific understanding. Concerns about risks are well founded, as has been demonstrated by studies on some GM crops and foods that have shown adverse effects on animal health and non-target organisms, indicated above. Many of these studies have, in fact, fed into the negotiation and/or implementation processes of the Cartagena Protocol and the Codex. We support the application of the Precautionary Principle with regard to the release and transboundary movement of GM crops and foods.

Conclusions

In the scope of this document, we can only highlight a few examples to illustrate that the totality of scientific research outcomes in the field of GM crop safety is nuanced; complex; often contradictory or inconclusive; confounded by researchers' choices, assumptions, and funding sources; and, in general, has raised more questions than it has currently answered.

Whether to continue and expand the introduction of GM crops and foods into the human food and animal feed supply, and whether the identified risks are acceptable or not, are decisions that involve socioeconomic considerations beyond the scope of a narrow scientific debate and the currently unresolved biosafety research agendas. These decisions must therefore involve the broader society. They should, however, be supported by strong scientific evidence on the long-term safety of GM crops and foods for human and animal health and the environment, obtained in a manner that is honest, ethical, rigorous, independent, transparent, and sufficiently diversified to compensate for bias.

Decisions on the future of our food and agriculture should not be based on misleading and misrepresentative claims by an internal circle of likeminded stakeholders that a "scientific consensus" exists on GMO safety.

This document was subsequently opened for endorsement by scientists from around the world in their personal (rather than institutional) capacities reflecting their personal views and based on their personal expertise. There is no suggestion that the views expressed in this statement represent the views or position of any institution or organization with which the individuals are affiliated. Qualifying criteria for signing the statement were deliberately selected to include scientists, physicians, social scientists, academics, and specialists in legal aspects and risk assessment of GM crops and foods. Scientist and academic signatories were requested to have qualifications from accredited institutions at the level of PhD or equivalent. Legal experts were requested to have at least a JD or equivalent. By December 2013, more than

300 people who met the strict qualification requirements had signed the statement. The statement was widely taken up in the media and reported in numerous outlets and evidence provided therein continues to be cited widely. In a time when there is major pressure on the science community from corporate and political interests, it is of utmost importance that scientists working for the public interest take a stand against attempts to reduce and compromise the rigour of examination of new applications in favor of rapid commercialization of new and emerging technologies that are expected to generate profit and economic growth. The document continues to be open for signature on the website of the initiating scientific organization ENSSER (European Network of Scientists for Social and Environmental Responsibility) at www. ensser.org.

Notes

1. Séralini GE, Clair E, Mesnage R, Gress S, Defarge N, Malatesta M, et al. Republished study: long-term toxicity of a Roundup herbicide and a Roundup-tolerant genetically modified maize. Environ Sci Eur. 2014;26(1):1.

2. Carman JA, Vlieger HR, Ver Steeg LJ, Sneller VE, Robinson GW, Clinch-Jones CA, et al. A long-term toxicology study on pigs fed a combined genetically modified (GM) soy and GM maize diet. J Org Syst. 2013;8(1):38–54.

3. Frewin G. (2013). The new "is GM food safe?" meme. Axis Mundi, 18 July. http://www.axismundionline.com/blog/the-new-is-gm-food-safe-meme/; Wikipedia (2013). Genetically modified food controversies. [http://en.wikipedia.org/wiki/Genetically_modified_food_controversies].

4. Lynas M: GMO pigs study—more junk science. Marklynas.org 2013, 12 June [http://www.marklynas.org/2013/06/gmo-pigs-study-more-junk-science/],

5. Kloor K: Greens on the run in debate over genetically modified food. Bloomberg 2013, 7 January [http://www.bloomberg.com/news/2013-01-07/green-activist-reverses-stance-on-genetically-modified-food.html],

6. White M: The scientific debate about GM foods is over: they're safe. Pacific Standard Magazine 2013, 24 September [http://www.psmag.com/health/scientific-debate-gm-foods-theyre-safe-66711/],

7. European Network of Scientists for Social and Environmental Responsibility ENSSER [www.ensser.org],

8. Domingo JL, Bordonaba JG. A literature review on the safety assessment of genetically modified plants. Environ Int. 2011;37:734–42.

9. Snell C, Bernheim A, Bergé JB, Kuntz M, Pascal G, Paris A, et al. Assessment of the health impact of GM plant diets in long-term and multigenerational animal feeding trials: a literature review. Food Chem Toxicol. 2012;50(3–4):1134–48.

10. Séralini GE, Mesnage R, Clair E, Gress S, Spiroux de Vendômois J, Cellier D. Genetically modified crops safety assessments: present limits and possible improvements. Environ Sci Eur. 2011;23:10.

11. Dona A, Arvanitoyannis IS. Health risks of genetically modified foods. Crit Rev Food Sci Nutr. 2009;49(2):164–75.

12. Diels J, Cunha M, Manaia C, Sabugosa-Madeira B, Silva M. Association of financial or professional conflict of interest to research outcomes on health risks or nutritional assessment studies of genetically modified products. Food Policy. 2011;36:197–203.

13. Séralini GE, Mesnage R, Defarge N, Gress S, Hennequin D, Clair E, et al. Answers to critics: why there is a long term toxicity due to NK603 Roundup-tolerant genetically modified maize and to a Roundup herbicide. Food Chem Toxicol. 2013;53:461–8.

14. EU Food Policy: Commission and EFSA agree need for two-year GMO feeding studies. 17 December 2012,

15. French Ministry of Ecology, Sustainable Development and Energy2013: Programme National de Recherche: Risques environnementaux et sanitaires liés aux OGM (Risk'OGM) 2013, 12 July [http://www.developpement-durable. gouv.fr/IMG/pdf/ APR__Risk_OGM_rel_pbch_pbj_rs2.pdf],

16. Wikipedia: Genetically modified food controversies. 2013 [http://en. wikipedia.org/ wiki/Genetically_modified_food_controversies],

17. Masip G: Opinion: Don't fear GM crops, Europe! The Scientist 2013, May 28 [http:// www.the-scientist.com/?articles.view/articleNo/35578/title/Opinion– Don-t-Fear-GM-Crops–Europe-/],

18. Royal Society of Canada: Elements of precaution: recommendations for the regulation of food biotechnology in Canada; An Expert Panel Report on the Future of Food Biotechnology. 2001, January [http://www.rsc.ca//files/ publications/expert_panels/ foodbiotechnology/GMreportEN.pdf],

19. British Medical Association Board of Science and Education: Genetically modified food and health: a second interim statement. 2004, March [http://bit.ly/19QAHSI],

20. American Medical Association House of Delegates: Labeling of bioengineered foods. Council on Science and Public Health Report 2, 2012 [http://www.amaassn.org/ resources/doc/csaph/a12-csaph2-bioengineeredfoods.pdf],

21. AAAS: Statement by the AAAS Board of Directors on labeling of genetically modified foods. 2012, 20 October. [http://www.aaas.org/news/releases/2012/ media/AAAS_GM_statement.pdf],

22. Hunt P, Blumberg B, Bornehag CG, Collins TJ, DeFur PL, Gilbert SG, et al. Yes: food labels would let consumers make informed choices. Environmental Health News 2012 [http://www.environmentalhealthnews.org/ehs/news/ 2012/yes-labels-on-gm-foods],

23. European Commission: A decade of EU-funded GMO research (2001–2010). 2010 [http://ec.europa.eu/research/biosociety/pdf/a_decade_of_eu-funded_gmo_research. pdf],

24. European Commission: A decade of EU-funded GMO research (2001–2010). 2010, 128. [http://ec.europa.eu/research/biosociety/pdf/a_decade_of_eufunded_gmo_ research.pdf],

25. European Commission: A decade of EU-funded GMO research (2001–2010). 2010, 157. [http://ec.europa.eu/research/biosociety/pdf/a_decade_of_eufunded_gmo_ research.pdf],

26. Tribe D: 600+ published safety assessments. GMOPundit blog undated [http:// gmopundit.blogspot.co.uk/p/450-published-safety-assessments.html] Hilbeck et al. Environmental Sciences Europe (2015) 27:4,

27. Brouk M, Cvetkovic B, Rice DW, Smith BL, Hinds MA, Owens FN, et al. Performance of lactating dairy cows fed corn as whole plant silage and grain produced from a genetically modified event DAS-59122-7 compared to a nontransgenic, near isoline control. J Dairy Sci. 2011;94:1961–6.

28. Calsamiglia S, Hernandez B, Hartnell GF, Phipps R. Effects of corn silage derived from a genetically modified variety containing two transgenes on feed intake, milk production, and composition, and the absence of detectable transgenic deoxyribonucleic acid in milk in Holstein dairy cows. J Dairy Sci. 2007;90:4718–23.

29. de Vendômois JS, Roullier F, Cellier D, Séralini GE. A comparison of the effects of three GM corn varieties on mammalian health. Int J Biol Sci. 2010;5(7):706–26.

30. Ewen SWB, Pusztai A. Effect of diets containing genetically modified potatoes expressing Galanthus nivalis lectin on rat small intestine. Lancet. 1999;354:1353–4.

31. Fares NH, El-Sayed AK. Fine structural changes in the ileum of mice fed on delta-endotoxin-treated potatoes and transgenic potatoes. Nat Toxins. 1998;6:219–33.

32. Kilic A, Akay MT. A three generation study with genetically modified Bt corn in rats: biochemical and histopathological investigation. Food Chem Toxicol. 2008;46(3):1164–70.

33. Malatesta M, Caporaloni C, Gavaudan S, Rocchi MB, Serafini S, Tiberi C, et al. Ultrastructural morphometrical and immunocytochemical analyses of hepatocyte nuclei from mice fed on genetically modified soybean. Cell Struct Funct. 2002;27:173–80.

34. Malatesta M, Biggiogera M, Manuali E, Rocchi MB, Baldelli B, Gazzanelli G. Fine structural analyses of pancreatic acinar cell nuclei from mice fed on genetically modified soybean. Eur J Histochem. 2003;47:385–8.

35. Hammond B, Dudek R, Lemen J, Nemeth M. Results of a 13 week safety assurance study with rats fed grain from glyphosate tolerant corn. Food Chem Toxicol. 2004;42(6):1003–14.

36. Hammond BG, Dudek R, Lemen J, Nemeth M. Results of a 90-day safety assurance study with rats fed grain from corn borer-protected corn. Food Chem Toxicol. 2006;44(7):1092–9.

37. Hilbeck A, Meier M, Römbke J, Jänsch S, Teichmann H, Tappeser B. Environmental risk assessment of genetically modified plants concepts and controversies. Environ Sci Eur. 2011;23:13.

38. Hilbeck A, Schmidt JEU. Another view on Bt proteins—how specific are they and what else might they do? Biopesti Int. 2006;2(1):1–50.

39. Székács A, Darvas B. Comparative aspects of Cry toxin usage in insect control. In: Ishaaya I, Palli SR, Horowitz AR, editors. Advanced Technologies for Managing Insect Pests. Dordrecht, Netherlands: Springer; 2012. p. 195–230.

40. Marvier M, McCreedy C, Regetz J, Kareiva P. A meta-analysis of effects of Bt cotton and maize on nontarget invertebrates. Science. 2007;316(5830):1475–7.

41. Lang A, Vojtech E. The effects of pollen consumption of transgenic Bt maize on the common swallowtail, Papilio machaon L. (Lepidoptera, Papilionidae). Basic Appl Ecol. 2006;7:296–306.

42. Gassmann AJ, Petzold-Maxwell JL, Keweshan RS, Dunbar MW. Field-evolved resistance to Bt maize by Western corn rootworm. PLoS One. 2011;6(7):e22629.

43. Zhao JH, Ho P, Azadi H. Benefits of Bt cotton counterbalanced by secondary pests? Perceptions of ecological change in China. Environ Monit Assess. 2010;173(1–4):985–94.

44. Lu Y, Wu K, Jiang Y, Xia B, Li P, Feng H, et al. Mirid bug outbreaks in multiple crops correlated with wide-scale adoption of Bt cotton in China. Science. 2010;328(5982):1151–4.

45. Benbrook C. Impacts of genetically engineered crops on pesticide use in the US—the first sixteen years. Environ Sci Eur. 2012;24:24.

46. Heinemann JA, Massaro M, Coray DS, Agapito-Tenfen SZ, Wen JD. Sustainability and innovation in staple crop production in the US Midwest. Int J Agric Sustainability. 2013;12:71–88.

47. Powles SB. Evolved glyphosate-resistant weeds around the world: lessons to be learnt. Pest Manag Sci. 2008;64:360–5.

48. Székács A, Darvas B: Forty years with glyphosate. Herbicides properties, synthesis and control of weeds. Hasaneen MN, InTech. 2012,

49. Benedetti D, Nunes E, Sarmento M, Porto C, dos Santos CEI, Dias JF, et al. Genetic damage in soybean workers exposed to pesticides: evaluation with the comet and buccal micronucleus cytome assays. Mutat Res. 2013;752(1–2):28–33.

50. Lopez SL, Aiassa D, Benitez-Leite S, Lajmanovich R, Manas F, Poletta G, et al. 2012: Pesticides used in South American GMO-based agriculture: a review of their effects on humans and animal models. Advances in Molecular Toxicology. Fishbein JC, Heilman JM. New York, Elsevier 2012, 6: 41–75.

51. Kvakkestad V, Gillund F, Kjolberg KA, Vatn A. Scientists perspectives on the deliberate release of GM crops. Environ Values. 2007;16(1):79–104.

52. Secretariat of the Convention on Biological Diversity: Cartagena Protocol on Biosafety to the Convention on Biological Diversity 2000 [http://bch.cbd.int/ protocol/text/],

53. Codex Alimentarius: Foods derived from modern biotechnology. 2d ed. World Health Organization/Food and Agriculture Organization of the United Nations 2000 [ftp://ftp.fao.org/codex/Publications/Booklets/Biotech/ Biotech_2009e.pdf],

"*The public debate around the safety of genetically modified organisms (GMOs) and whether to label them has continued to rage.*"

Consumption of GE Crops Shows No Adverse Effects

Kelly Servick

In the following viewpoint, Kelly Servick states that the GE foods in commercial production show no evidence of adverse effects. Reporting that the research retreads previously given conclusions on the safety of GE crops, she turns the discussion toward regulatory issues for new biotechnology products. Servick is a staff writer at Science who focuses on stories about biomedical research and policy. She studied science writing at the University of California, Santa Cruz, and her work has appeared in Wired, Scientific American, and other outlets.

As you read, consider the following questions:

1. What does data show about health problems and GE crops?
2. How is the new CRISPR technology different from the first wave of gene-editing technology?
3. What approach should be used to determine when a full safety review is necessary for biotechnology products?

Almost 2 years ago, a group of 20 scientists began hashing out a consensus on the risks and benefits of genetically engineered (GE) crops. Since the launch of their study, sponsored by the National Academies of Science, Engineering, and Medicine, the public debate around the safety of genetically modified organisms (GMOs) and whether to label them has continued to rage. But behind the scenes, some things have changed. Agricultural markets are now bracing for an explosion of new plants designed using the precise gene-editing technology CRISPR, and regulators in both the United States and the European Union are struggling with how to assess their safety.

The panel's report, released today, is a hefty literature review that tackles mainstay questions in the well-worn GMO debate. Are these plants safe to eat? How do they affect the environment? Do they drive herbicide-resistance in weeds or pesticide-resistance in insects? But it also weighs in on a more immediate conundrum for federal agencies: what to do with gene-edited plants that won't always fit the technical definition of a regulated GE crop.

The authors picked through hundreds of research papers to make generalizations about GE varieties already in commercial production: There is "reasonable evidence that animals were not harmed by eating food derived from GE crops," and epidemiological data shows no increase in cancer or any other health problems as a result of these crops entering into our food supply. Pest-resistant crops that poison insects thanks to a gene from the soil bacterium *Bacillus thuringiensis* (Bt) generally allow farmers to use less pesticide. Farmers can manage the risk of those pests evolving resistance by using crops with high enough levels of the toxin and planting non-Bt "refuges" nearby. Crops designed to be resistant to the herbicide glyphosate, meanwhile, can lead to heavy reliance on the chemical, and spawn resistant weeds that "present a major agronomic problem." The panel urges more research on strategies to delay weed resistance.

Few researchers will be surprised at those conclusions, says Todd Kuiken, who leads the Synthetic Biology Project at the

Woodrow Wilson International Center for Scholars, a think tank in Washington, DC, but public skepticism of GE crops runs deep. "Whether the academy kind of putting their seal of approval on that impacts the discussion, I don't know."

Regulatory Muddle

The report saves the issue of regulation for its final chapter. Many countries—including the United States, whose framework for reviewing new biotechnology products was drafted in 1986—didn't envision modern technologies when they legally defined genetic engineering. The first generation of GE crops used a bacterium to ferry genes from one organism into another. But CRISPR can knockout or precisely edit DNA sequences without leaving behind any foreign DNA. In fact, the DNA of a gene-edited crop could end up looking nearly identical to that of a conventionally bred variety. Last month, the US Department of Agriculture (USDA) deemed two CRISPR-edited crops, a mushroom that resists browning and a high-yield variety of waxy corn, to be exempt from its review process because neither contained genetic material from species considered to be "plant pests."

Critics of those decisions argue that small genetic changes can still have big effects on the characteristics of a plant, and that gene-edited crops have slipped through the cracks without proper safety testing. Others argue that the precision of CRISPR limits environmental and health risks by making fewer unintended tweaks to a plant's genome, and that subjecting them to a full regulatory review is needlessly costly and time consuming for their producers.

Last summer, the White House announced it would revamp the legal framework for evaluating biotechnology products across USDA, the Food and Drug Administration, and the Environmental Protection Agency (EPA). The European Commission, meanwhile, is also mulling whether plants without foreign DNA count as genetically modified.

GMO FOOD: THE BENEFITS AND CONTROVERSIES

So what are the benefits of GMOs? According to the Office of Science at the US Department of Energy, one of the pros of genetically modified crops is a better taste, increased nutrients, resistance to disease and pests, and faster output of crops.

The Food and Agriculture Organization of the United Nations also says that farmers can grow more food on less land with genetically modified crops.

Genetically modified animals have certain genes inserted into their genomes so that they can produce "better" milk, eggs, and meat. These animals also are expected to have a higher resistance to disease and overall better health, with better natural waste management. In theory, genetically modified crops and animals will also be more environmentally friendly because they conserve water, soil, and energy.

The Food and Agriculture Organization of the United Nations states that one of the positives of GMOs is that farmers can produce more nutritious food. Many foods are in the works for bio-fortification for this reason. Rice, for example, feeds 50 percent of the world's population, so genetically modifying rice to have more vitamin A would reduce vitamin A deficiency in developing countries.

But what happens to these plants and animals that have been genetically modified? What happens when we eat these foods? Unfortunately, no one knows for sure what happens, though evidence is mounting that genetic modification may not be a good thing.

The Office of Science at the US Department of Energy also lists some of the controversies associated with genetically modified foods. One of these controversies are the potential health risks, including allergies, antibiotic resistance, and unknown effects. Other negatives that stem from GMOs is that scientists are tampering with nature by mixing genes and no one knows what this is doing to the animals or the environment.

"Genetically Modified Organisms: Pros and Cons of GMO Food," by Janelle Vaesa, Decoded Science, January 5, 2013.

Like several National Academies reviews before it, the new study condemned regulatory approaches that classify products based on the technology used to create them. "The National Academy has been saying since 1987 that it should be the product, not the process," says Fred Gould, an applied evolutionary biologist at North Carolina State University in Raleigh, and chair of the new report. "But the problem up until now is … how do you decide which products need more examination than others?"

There, the report makes a new suggestion: Regulators should ask for a full analysis of a plant's composition—using modern "-omics" tools such as genome sequencing and analysis of the proteins and small molecules in a sample—to determine when a full safety review is necessary. The authors propose that crops containing different genes, producing a different set of proteins, or carrying out different metabolic reactions than conventionally bred varieties should trigger regulatory review if those differences have potential health or environmental impacts. And if a trait is so new that there's no conventional counterpart to compare it to … just go ahead and regulate it, they conclude.

The approach is reasonable, Kuiken says, but it's not clear how to implement it. "How close does it have to be to the counterpart before you have to do a full review?"

Gould acknowledges that the report's recommendation is a tall order, but "if USDA and EPA don't use -omics techniques and they deregulate a crop, and then somebody in a research lab just takes a look at the transcriptome and finds a difference, you're in trouble." Deciding exactly which kinds of genetic or metabolic changes represent a risk will be left to regulatory agencies. "We just give principles," Gould adds. "We're not in the trenches with them."

If those entrenched regulators crave more guidance, they're in luck. The National Academies just launched yet another study, due out by the end of this year, to predict the next decade of biotechnology products and describe the scientific tools needed to regulate them.

> "Most people who are concerned
> about modern biotechnology have
> little or no knowledge of the processes
> that have been used to transform
> crops in the past. Nor are they
> likely aware that crops have been
> continually altered over time or that,
> without human care, they would
> cease to exist."

Plant Evolution Has Been Occurring Since Before Gene-Editing Technology

American Society of Plant Biologists

In the following viewpoint, excerpted for length, the American Society of Plant Biologists (ASPB) argues that humans have been altering plants since agriculture evolved, well before modern biotechnology was developed. The ASPB claims that we have always lacked information about our food even with classically bred crops, and that in comparison, we know more with GM foods. Formerly known as the American Society of Plant Physiologists, the ASPB is a professional society dedicated to advancing the plant sciences. The ASPB publishes two world-class journals, Plant Physiology *and* The Plant Cell.

As you read, consider the following questions:

1. According to the viewpoint, how has human intervention changed domesticated crops from their wild progenitors?
2. According to the viewpoint, what tools have scientists used across time to develop better crop varieties?
3. According to the viewpoint, in what ways have we always lived with food risks?

[…]

Agriculture evolved independently in many places on this earth, but the earliest evidence of farming dates 10,000 years ago in present day Iraq (Heiser, 1990). For much of the 200,000 or so years prior to agriculture, humans lived as nomadic hunters, gatherers, and scavengers surviving solely on wild plants and animals. Subsequent domestication of these wild plants and animals from their natural habitats launched agriculture, thus radically transforming human societies. This occurred initially in the Fertile Crescent, the Andean region in South America, Mexico, and parts of Asia, but diffused throughout much of the globe. A change from the nomadic lifestyle to farming led us to become community dwellers, eventually spawning the development of languages, literature, science, and technology as people were freed from the continuous daily task of finding food. Some regions caught on much faster than others, by margins of thousands of years (Diamond, 1999).

Plants have also evolved or, more accurately, they have been changed rapidly by human intervention (Harlan, 1992). Every crop plant grown today is related to a wild species occurring naturally in its center of origin, and progenitors of many of our crops are still found in the wild. Early humans must have tried eating thousands of feral plant species from a pool of a quarter of a million flowering plants before settling down on less than one thousand such species, which were subsequently tamed and adapted to farming. A little over 100 crop species are now grown intensively around the world, with only a handful of them supplying us with most of what we now eat. Through a process of gradual selection, our ancestors chose a very tiny section of the wild plant community and transformed it into cultivated crops. Some profound alterations in the plant phenotype occurred during such selection, and these include determinate growth habit; elimination of grain shattering; synchronous ripening; shorter maturity; reduction of bitterness and harmful toxins; reduced seed dispersal, sprouting and dormancy; greater productivity, including bigger seed or fruit size; and even an elimination of seeds, such as in banana. These changes reduced the survivability of crops in the wild, and thus a feature that transcends all of our crops is the reduction of weedy traits from wild plants. Present crops are thus totally dependent upon human care for their survival, and modern crop varieties would persist in the wild "no longer than a Chihuahua would last in the company of wolves" (Trewavas, 2000).

Most crops that supply our food were thus obtained at the end of the Stone Age, often from a relatively narrow pool of extant wild genetic diversity. Additional diversity arose within such cultivated crops through new mutations and natural hybridization, and through judicious selection and perpetuation by farmers who maintained them as land races. Varied uses and preferences brought forth further diversification such as in corn (popcorn, sweet corn, dent corn, broom corn, and flour corn for tortilla and corn bread) or the derivatives of ancestral cabbage (kale, kohl rabi, brussels sprouts, cabbage, cauliflower, and broccoli).

With the advent of transoceanic navigation and the "discovery" of the New World, crops were moved around the world rapidly, often achieving prominence in adopted homes far beyond their natural centers of origin or domestication. For instance, the United States is the leading producer of corn and soybean in the word, yet these crops are native to Mexico and China, respectively. The world's largest traded commodity, coffee, had a humble origin in Ethiopia, but now much of it is produced in Latin America and Asia. Florida oranges have their roots in India, while sugarcane arose in Papua New Guinea. Food crops that are now so integral to the culture or diet in the Old World, such as the potato in Europe, chili pepper in India, cassava in Africa, and sweet potato in Japan, were introduced from South America. For that matter, every crop in North America other than the blueberry, Jerusalem artichoke, sunflower, and squash are borrowed from elsewhere!

A few sources of our food are also recent domesticates. Chinese gooseberry occurs wildly in China and is not edible. But careful breeding made it palatable, and it was re-christened "Kiwi fruit" in New Zealand after its introduction there early in the 20th century. The modern strawberry with big fruits is a product of the accidental crossing of two wild species from Virginia (United States) and Chile in France in the mid-18th century. Rapeseed, grown in India for centuries, was altered recently through classical breeding to eliminate the toxic erucic acid and smelly glucosinolates to result in canola—Canadian oil. Triticale, a completely new crop, was artificially sythesized a few decades ago by combining the genomes of wheat and rye (two distinct genera that do not interbreed in nature). It is now grown on over three million acres worldwide. Modern bread wheat itself is also a fairly recent crop in the evolutionary time scale, having arisen only about 4,000 years ago through hybridization of tetraploid (pasta or durum) wheat with inedible goat grass.

From Mesopotamia to Mendel

While humans have always molded the evolution of crop plants, such changes imposed by farmers occurred over several millennia, leading to rich crop diversity—especially in traits related to their planting or consumption. At the same time, global population grew very slowly until the mid-19th century. It took 1,800 years for the global population to climb from an estimated 300 million around the time when Christianity began, to reach its first billion. But it took only 12 years to add the last billion, rising from five billion people in 1987 to six billion two years ago.

Fortunately, parallel scientific developments in agriculture ensured that food production kept pace with the population explosion of the past century (Conway, 1999). Beginning with Mendel's study of peas, knowledge of genetics helped usher in scientific crop development, resulting in high-yielding varieties. Food production increased in every part of the world in the past few decades, including in Africa. Per capita food consumption has also increased steadily everywhere except in parts of sub-Saharan Africa. In the United States and Canada, where such scientific developments and their applications were most intense, one average farmer now produces enough to feed nearly 150 people! In crops subject to intensive scientific attention—corn, wheat, and rice—the productivity levels increased severalfold. For example, US corn growers averaged 26 bushels of corn per acre in 1928 and 134 bushels per acre in 1998 (National Corn Growers Association, 2001).

Such a prodigious increase in agricultural production was underpinned by scientific crop improvement methods along with other developments, including the use of irrigation, improved soil fertility management, mechanization, and control of diseases and pests (Conway, 1999). To develop better crop varieties, scientists have used an array of tools. Artificial crossing, or hybridization, helped us assimilate desirable traits from several varieties into elite cultivars. When desired characteristics were unavailable in the cultivated plants, genes were liberally borrowed from wild relatives and introduced into crop plants. When a crop variety refused to mate with the wild species, various tricks were employed to force them to intermingle, such as the use of the carcinogenic chemical colchicine or by rescuing the hybrid embryos with tissue culture methods. Hybrid vigor was exploited in crops such as corn and cotton to boost productivity. When existing genetic variation within the cultivated germplasm was not adequate, breeders created new variants using ionizing irradiation (gamma ray, x-ray, neutron), mutagenic chemicals (ethyl methane sulfate, mustard gas), or through somaclonal variation (cell culture).

Most people who are concerned about modern biotechnology have little or no knowledge of the processes that have been used to transform crops in the past. Nor are they likely aware that crops have been continually altered over time or that, without human care, they would cease to exist. Using a variety of tools over the past few decades, plant breeders have radically transformed our crop plants by altering their architecture (such as the development of dwarf wheat and rice), shortening growing seasons, developing greater resistance to diseases and pests (all crops), and developing bigger seeds and fruits ... These crops are also more responsive to management and better adapted to diverse ecological conditions. Improved food quality also resulted through fewer toxins (canola), better digestibility (beans), increased nutrition (high-protein corn), better taste, longer shelf life (thus withstanding long transportation and storage), and enhanced freshness in many vegetables and fruits. A 1,000-fold increase in the marble-sized wild Lycopersicon resulted in the modern tomato that can now weigh as much as a kilogram (Frary and Tanksley, 2000).

Modern farming has steadily increased the supply of relatively safe, affordable, and abundant food not only in the developed world, but also in most developing countries. An average American family now spends only 11% of its income on food and yet has access to better food choices with more variety and nutrition than ever before. Without scientific developments in agriculture, we would otherwise be farming on every square inch of arable land to produce the same amount of food!

Using gene transfer techniques to develop GM crops thus can be seen as a logical extension of the continuum of devices we have used to amend our crop plants for millennia. When compared to the gross genetic alterations using wide-species hybridization or the use of mutagenic irradiation, direct introduction of one or a few genes into crops results in subtle and less disruptive changes that are relatively specific and predictable. The process is also clearly more expeditious, as the development of new cultivars by classical breeding typically takes from 10 to 15 years. The primary attraction of the gene transfer methods to the plant breeder, however, is the opportunity to tap into a wide gene pool to borrow traits, obviating the constraints of cross-compatible crop species.

Addressing Public Concerns

While direct gene transfer is still a relatively new approach, many concerns arising from its use may be addressed with the "benchmark" of conventionally bred varieties, as we have the accumulated experience and knowledge with the latter for more than a century. While it seems logical to express a concern such as "I don't know what I am eating with GM foods!" it must be remembered that we really never had that information before with classically bred crops. With GM crops, at least we know what new genetic material is being introduced, so we can test for predictable and even many unpredictable effects. Consider, for example, how conventional plant breeders would develop a disease-resistant tomato. They would introduce chromosome fragments from its wild relative to add a gene for disease resistance. In the process, hundreds of unknown and unwanted genes would also be introduced, with the risk that some of them could encode toxins or allergens, armaments that wild plants deploy to survive. Yet we never routinely tested most conventionally bred varieties for food safety or environmental risk factors, and they were not subject to any regulatory oversight. We have always lived with food risks, but in the last few decades we have become increasingly more adept at asking questions.

To address the concern about long-term health consequences of GM foods, it is instructive to recognize that we worried little about such impacts when massive amounts of new proteins (and unfamiliar chemicals) were introduced into our foods from wild species or when unknown changes were created through mutation breeding. When new foods from exotic crops are introduced, we often assimilate them easily into our diets. What's more we rarely, if ever, before asked the same questions that we now pose about GM crops. Many so-called functional foods, health foods, and nutraceuticals have been entering into the mainstream American diet lately, with little or no regulation or testing. We do not question the long-term health implications of these food supplements, even though they involve relatively large changes in our food intake. In contrast, the GM foods currently on the market have been tested extensively and judged to be substantially equivalent to their conventional counterparts, with just one or two additional proteins present in miniscule amounts (introduced into a background of thousands of proteins). And, those proteins are broken down either during processing or digestion, with little long-term consequence. In food products such as oil, starch, and sugar, such proteins are not even found. A nagging potential problem with a new protein in food is that it could be a potential allergen. As most food allergens are now well studied, we know that they are found in few defined sources (peanut and other grain legumes, shellfish, tree nuts, and a handful of other foods) and share many similar structural features. Moreover, they must be present in huge proportions in our food, and we must be sensitized to them over time for them to cause any adverse effects. Thus, it is highly unlikely for new allergens to be introduced into our food supply from GM plants.

[...]

> *"A special feature of GM breeding is that it allows the transfer into crop plants of one or a few genes from what might be radically different organisms. Conventional breeding cannot, for example, form plants that can assemble complex human immunoglobulins as has been achieved in GM plants."*

Gene-Editing Has Major Difference from Conventional Plant Evolution

Nathanael Johnson

In the following viewpoint, Nathanael Johnson investigates the difference between genetic engineering and natural breeding. He asserts that conventional breeding is not as gradual and naturalistic as the public may imagine and that some of the risks associated with genetic engineering occur naturally in the wild as well. However, he notes that there is a potentially important difference concerning gene transference between radically different organisms. Johnson is a journalist and senior food writer for Grist. *He has taught in the Graduate School of Journalism at the University of California, Berkeley, and written two books.*

"Genetic Engineering vs. Natural Breeding: What's the Difference?" by Nathanael Johnson, Grist Magazine, Inc., July 16, 2013. Reprinted by permission.

As you read, consider the following questions:

1. According to the viewpoint, how does conventional breeding work?
2. According to the viewpoint, why are genetically engineered foods screened for potential allergens?
3. What double standard does Johnson encourage readers to be thoughtful about?

If you are new to this series, I've been trying to break down the competing claims about genetic engineering. I'm not an expert: When I told a friend I was writing about GMOs he asked, "So are you for them, or against?" My answer: "I'm trying to figure that out."

The next step in trying to figure that out is to really understand how genetic engineering works. Is this process simply a minor extension of plant-breeding techniques? Or is there a way in which genetic engineering represents a fundamental discontinuity with the age-old practice of farmers selecting seeds?

That's what I asked Pamela Ronald, a scientist at UC Davis who uses genetic engineering to study rice. I approached Ronald because she's not one of those scientists who is so used to looking through the microscope that she loses sight of the big ecological picture. Her husband, Raoul Adamchack, teaches organic agriculture at Davis, and together they wrote the book *Tomorrow's Table*, which makes the case for incorporating genetic engineering into organic practices. Nor is Ronald among the progress-addled optimists who rush to embrace every new technology. She gave birth to her third child in her outdoor hot tub, because the science suggests that—for a normal pregnancy, with one kid already out, and a hospital nearby—it's actually safer.

When I started to ask questions, Ronald asked if we could back up a bit. "I end up asking people, 'What is it that bothers you about genetic engineering?'" she said. "Is it the idea of moving genes from one species to another? Well, what we do here is rice—we put rice genes into rice plants. Is it that you don't like corporations? Well,

I'm at a university here, and we're funded by the government. Is it that you don't like profits? Well, we have no private funding, and the rice we are developing is all for developing countries. We don't make money off our discoveries."

What bothers me about genetically engineered crops, I told her, is that the technology seems to disrupt the co-evolutionary relationship between farmer and plant. I like the idea of farmers saving seeds and coaxing plants toward a greater harmony with their environment (the seasons, the pests, the culture), rather than buying their seeds each year from Monsanto. Plus, in that slow process of selection, it might be easier to weed out any unintended effects that cause problems.

"So," she said, "in the developed world almost everyone buys their seeds, but the people using our rice can't afford that. They need to self their seeds" (i.e., they self-pollinate their seeds each year to provide for the next).

In the US farmers buy hybrid seeds, which don't work as well if you try to save the next generation. But the farmers in Bangladesh, who use rice Ronald pioneered, save seeds every year. The seeds are genetically engineered, yes are breed to contain genes discovered with GE—but then they continue that process of co-evolutionary selection. As for the risk of unintended problems, Ronald said, "Any time you introduce a new seed there's some risk, but the risks are small and the benefits are huge. I just think we need to work with whatever technology works best to achieve the goals of sustainable agriculture."

As with birth, it's a question of appropriate technology. I wanted to see for myself what it meant to create new seed, and how we might parse the risks of the various methods for doing it. The next day I drove up to Davis. Ronald was traveling, so she left me in the care of Randy Ruan, her lab tech.

Ruan told me to meet him outside the greenhouse. He'd leaned a red bicycle (with an Obama button pined to a pannier) against the glass. He seemed a little bemused by my interest.

"Take as many pictures of rice as you like," he said.

He had a point. Everything pretty much looked like rice. But the story behind each plant was slightly different.

When doing marker-assisted breeding, scientists cross their plants through pollination, hoping to get an exciting new combination of traits. As new plants emerge, they can take a tiny piece of tissue and see if it contains the genes they were hoping for. If not, they can discard the plants. It's conventional breeding, assisted by a keyhole through which to peek at the DNA.

The problem with conventional breeding, marker-assisted or otherwise, is that it's messy, said Margaret Smith, a plant breeder at Cornell. (I followed up with her to fill in the nitty gritty of how things worked.) You're mixing two whole strands of DNA and swapping lots of genes at once, Smith explained. Researchers crossbreed generation after generation with a plant that displays an interesting mutation, creating thousands of plants, most of which they will destroy. It's not exactly the slow dance with the land that I'd imagined.

Another way to tweak crops is to induce mutations by dousing seeds in mutagenic chemicals or zapping them with radiation. This causes bits of DNA to copy incorrectly, which causes more changes than you generally see with genetic engineering. "You're just rolling the dice and hoping to get something interesting," Smith said.

It works. As it turns out, the 20-pound bag of organic brown rice on top of my refrigerator was a strain (Calrose 76) that mutated after exposure to 25 kR of Cobalt-60 gamma radiation.

The most common mode of experimentation in Ronald's lab, of course, is genetic engineering. Ruan gamely pointed out a few examples. Ronald had mentioned that there were two main projects for which her lab is known: the discovery of the gene XA21, which confers resistance to bacterial disease—good for farmers in the developing world who can't afford antibacterial pesticides; and a gene that allows rice to tolerate submergence better—good for those same farmers, who now have an herbicide-free way of drowning weeds without drowning the rice.

There are two main ways of genetically engineering plants: shooting them with a gene gun, or using the microbe Agrobacterium tumefaciens. A gene gun literally shoots pellets coated with DNA through plant tissue. As a result of this pure mechanical force, a few genes end up in the nucleus and are incorporated into it. Ronald's lab, however, uses Agrobacterium. With a little arm twisting, I got Ruan to take me to the lab and walk me through the process.

I wanted to understand in detail how this worked because, years ago, I had attended a lecture given by Ignacio Chapela, a critic of genetic engineering, and his critique had turned on these details. Genetic engineers often make it sound as if they are cutting and pasting DNA in precise places, he said, but the genes are sprayed into the genome at random. The thing that really bothered Chapela is that scientists bundle the gene they want with several others: They will build a sequence starting with a promoter (or "on switch"), then the gene they want to transfer, then a marker (which displays some visible trait to show them everything is working), and a terminator (the "off switch").

Throw all this at a genome and it could cause trouble: The terminator sequence could break off, Chapela pointed out, and all of a sudden the plant is expressing not just the trait you want, but also whatever comes right after that in the genome. Plants often have inactive genes for the manufacture of toxins, for instance, and the randomness of genetic engineering could turn them on.

All this, it turns out, is absolutely true. But it's also occurring all the time in the wild and in plant breeding, without the assistance of genetic engineering. The process for building the bundle of genes is, in actuality, incredibly precise. Because researchers are working with a relatively small amount of DNA, they really can cut and paste with precision. To this sequence, they add a bit of DNA called a plasmid—which catches both ends of the sequence, turning it into a circle. Plasmids are strange and fascinating things: They are essentially tools that bacteria use to swap genetic information between species—an instrument for creating transgenics built by evolution.

Next comes Agrobacterium. This particular microbe specializes in injecting plasmids into plant DNA. In the wild it does this with genes that make the plant form a home in which the Agrobacterium thrive. Scientists simply replace those plasmids with the ones they've constructed.

Chapela was correct to say that this part of the process is random; there's no control over where the Agrobacterium insert their payload, and there is a chance that this bundle of DNA can fracture. But, Smith told me, the same thing happens during normal breeding. The promoter might, certainly, turn on unwanted genes. But the promoter, which almost always comes from the cauliflower mosaic virus, is doing the same thing all the time in the wild.

The difference, Chapela had hypothesized, was that genetic engineering methods would lead genes to fall into more vulnerable and unstable sections of the genome. But that hasn't happened. Analyses of thousands of genomes show that introduced genes fall randomly amid the DNA strands. The genes introduced by humans have proven to be no more likely to break up or move around the genome. (I'm not getting to Chapela's main point, that engineered genes were spreading with pollen. More on that later.)

Of course, Chapela's objection was just one possible scenario—others have and will continue to be raised. The point is, it's easy to overestimate the risk of the new while underestimating the risks of the status quo. Species appear to be fairly stable, but beneath the surface, we live in a churning ocean of genetic flux.

In 2003, when the United Kingdom's GM Science Review Panel (chaired by climate hawk Sir David King) looked closely at this issue, it concluded that genetic engineering was no more likely to produce unintended consequences than conventional breeding:

Conventional plant breeding can produce gross undirected and unpredictable genetic changes and in that sense has considerable uncertainty. This is well documented and we know much about the types of change at a cellular level.

There is, of course, one potentially important difference:

> A special feature of GM breeding is that it allows the transfer into crop plants of one or a few genes from what might be radically different organisms. Conventional breeding cannot, for example, form plants that can assemble complex human immunoglobulins as has been achieved in GM plants. This inevitably raises uncertainty about whether there are any novel genetic interactions and whether these are potentially harmful …
>
> A further special feature of GM breeding is that the products of particular gene constructs may become present in radically different foodstuffs, effectively independently of any biological relationships … this can hold important implications for risk management policy in areas such as the avoidance of exposures to any allergens that might pass through regulatory screening.

As a result, genetically engineered foods are screened for potential allergens. It's frequently pointed out that Pioneer Hi-Bred mistakenly introduced an allergen into soybeans when it added a gene from Brazil nuts. The rest of the story is that we know about this because there was the right testing regime, and the product never went on the market—the company (and the regulators) knew what to look for and successfully weeded the plant out.

So what's the takeaway of all this? Before I finished up my conversation with Margaret Smith, I asked her if there might be some evolutionary wisdom in the way genetic material gets swapped during normal reproduction that was fundamentally different than techniques of genetic engineering. We don't know of any, she said. But she added:

> I think we need to be thoughtful, and as we learn more we need to continue to think about this carefully. We're learning more every day—just look at the revolution in epigenetics—and that could change the way we approach this. But my message on this is that we shouldn't just stop because there are unknowns. Every technology has unknowns. We just have to be as thoughtful as we can.

Those of us who are suspicious of genetically engineered foods need to be thoughtful, too. It makes no sense, for instance, to protest GMOs while accepting that irradiated organic mutants should be exempt from any special regulation. It makes no sense to try to ban all genetically engineered foods if we aren't concerned about the rice-to-rice transfers that people like Ronald are doing.

I still think that we have an important role to play in making sure the technology isn't used inappropriately. But it's not useful to flail blindly against something we don't understand.

Update: Pamela Ronald made it clear during our initial conversation that, while she used genetic engineering for gene discovery, it was her collaborators, using marker-assisted selection who actually developed rice for farmers. I omitted this because I thought that a discussion of the distinction between basic and applied science would be tangential to the main point: How is GE different from conventional breeding?

This distinction, however, raises another important question, namely: Is genetic engineering actually a useful tool for sustainable agriculture? I'll be getting to that.

I did make one real mistake. Ronald's lab found the submergence tolerance gene Sub1, which is indeed the gene that was released in the Bangladeshi varieties, but it was introduced through marker-assisted selection. I regret the error.

Periodical and Internet Sources Bibliography

The following articles have been selected to supplement the diverse views presented in this chapter.

Omri Ben-Shahar, "The Environmentalist Case in Favor of GMO Food," *Forbes,* February 26, 2018. https://www.forbes.com/sites/omribenshahar/2018/02/26/the-environmentalist-case-in-favor-of-gmo-food/#723e967137de

Jane Brody, "Are G.M.O. Foods Safe?" *New York Times,* April 23, 2018. https://www.nytimes.com/2018/04/23/well/eat/are-gmo-foods-safe.html?rref=collection%2Ftimestopic%2FGenetically%20Modified%20Food

Joseph Erbentraut, "We're Asking the Wrong Questions about GMOS," *The Huffington Post,* January 26, 2017. https://www.huffingtonpost.com/entry/gmos-food-safety-debate_us_5888db76e4b061cf898c1a56

Maggie Fox, "Genetically Modified Crops Are Safe, Report Says," *NBC News,* May 17, 2016. https://www.nbcnews.com/health/health-news/genetically-modified-crops-are-safe-report-says-n575436

Tamar Haspel, "The Truth about Organic Produce and Pesticides," *The Washington Post,* May 21, 2018. https://www.washingtonpost.com/lifestyle/food/the-truth-about-organic-produce-and-pesticides/2018/05/18/8294296e-5940-11e8-858f-12becb4d6067_story.html?utm_term=.869e43d5dc4d

Michael Nedelman, "Pesticides: How 'Bout Washing Them Apples?" *CNN,* October 25, 2017. https://www.cnn.com/2017/10/25/health/apples-pesticides-wash-study/index.html

Arthur Neslen, "Glyphosate Shown to Disrupt Microbiome 'At Safe Levels,' Study Claims," *The Guardian,* May 16, 2018. https://www.theguardian.com/environment/2018/may/16/glyphosate-shown-to-disrupt-microbiome-at-safe-levels-study-claims

Alice Park, "Pesticides in Produce Linked to Women Not Getting Pregnant with IVF," *Time,* October 30, 2017. http://time.com/5000869/pesticide-fruits-vegetables-ivf/

CHAPTER 4

Do Pesticides and GMOs Need Stricter Regulation?

Chapter Preface

As GMO products increasingly populate the shelves in our supermarkets, so does the demand for more regulation rise. From a psychological perspective, people are predisposed to find natural things positive and the unnatural negative. GMOs, the product of humans intervening with nature in complex ways with consequences that the average consumer is only vaguely aware of, undoubtedly qualify as unnatural. Accordingly, uncertainty or even distrust is a common reaction. Concerned with the possibility of health risks and wanting the right to knowingly choose, many consumers desire upfront transparency about whether their food was genetically modified or not and call for the labeling of all GMO products.

However, if transparency is the goal, the solution may not be simply sticking on labels to every GM product. If not undertaken carefully, labeling can mislead and confuse consumers more than the absence of labels would have. Additionally, labeling GMO products can unintentionally perpetuate suspicions and stigmatize them despite there being no conclusive scientific evidence that GMOs can cause health issues in humans.

The demand for increased regulations relates to the safety testing of GMOs as well. Under the guidelines of the Food and Drug Administration (FDA), the safety testing of genetically modified foods is technically voluntary, and self-reported by the companies who developed the GMO. In practice, however, safety testing is understood to be obligatory, as GM products won't be cleared by the FDA without it, and companies do not risk not complying with the FDA's request for testing. However, anti-GMO groups raise concerns about the objectivity and thoroughness of this testing system and consider it insufficient.

The following chapter examines the debate around GMO labeling and testing in addition to the claim that pesticides need better management as well.

| "When health and environmental costs are factored in, pesticide application is only economical at a much lower threshold than what is commonly practiced."

Better Management of Pesticides Is Needed

Frank Eyhorn, Tina Roner, and Heiko Specking

In the following viewpoint, Frank Eyhorn, Tina Roner, and Heiko Specking argue that a great deal of pesticide usage is excessive and uneconomical in both industrialized and developing countries. The authors claim that Integrated Pest Management (IPM) shows that better management practices can reduce the use of pesticides without substantial loss in crop yields or increased costs. Eyhorn is an environmental scientist and senior advisor of sustainable agriculture at Helvetas. Roner was an advisor of sustainable agriculture at Helvetas. Specking is an analyst and advocate for sustainability.

As you read, consider the following questions:

1. According to the viewpoint, what measures can be taken to reduce acute pesticide poisoning?
2. According to the viewpoint, what are the external costs of pesticides in terms of health and environment?
3. According to the viewpoint, what is important to assess when considering whether or not to use pesticides?

"Reducing Pesticide Use and Risks—What Action Is Needed?" by Frank Eyhorn, Tina Roner and Heiko Specking, Helvetas Swiss Intercooperation, September 2015. Reprinted by permission.

Pesticides are used to protect crops and livestock from various pests, diseases, competition from weeds and parasites, thus contributing to increased agricultural production. They help farmers to reduce production costs and risks, and to survive in a highly competitive market. Global pesticide use has grown over the past 20 years to 3.5 billion kg active ingredients per year, amounting to a global market worth $45 billion.[1] A significant portion of the chemicals applied has proved to be excessive, uneconomic or unnecessary both in industrialized and developing countries.[2] While some countries reduced pesticide use over the past two decades (particularly UK, France, Denmark and Japan), in most regions it considerably increased.[1] In Switzerland, pesticide sales are more or less stable at 2'120 tons of active ingredients in 2013.[3] The volume alone, however, does not necessarily reflect the impact of pesticides used, as older products are often replaced by substances that have more effect at lower doses.

What Type of Pesticides Are Used

Herbicides account for 42%, insecticides 27%, fungicides 22% and disinfectants and other agrochemicals 9% of global pesticide sales. In Switzerland, fungicides have the highest share (47%), followed by herbicides (35%) and insecticides (17%).[3] Herbicides dominate the North American and European domestic markets where they are also used to synchronize ripening of crops, but insecticides are more commonly used elsewhere in the world.[1] Pesticide use intensity is highest in vegetable, fruit and cotton production.

Today's most used herbicide glyphosate was introduced in combination with genetically modified herbicide-tolerant (HT) crops in the late 1990s. Presently, glyphosate formulations (e.g. Roundup) account for more than 50% of total herbicide use[4] and are applied on more than 80% of the genetically modified crops.[5] The use of herbicides allows for methods like low- and zero-tillage that reduce soil erosion. However, serious concerns are increasingly raised due to the development of herbicide-resistant weeds.

Pesticides and Health

Pesticides can have adverse effects to human health—acute but also chronic. While there are no accurate data available on acute pesticide poisoning due to occupational and accidental exposure most estimates are in the range of several million cases per year.[6] Acute pesticide poisoning is a serious problem in developing countries and emerging economies, where many farmers use highly hazardous products, often without adequate protective measures. The harms in actual conditions of use are experienced disproportionately by the poor and disadvantaged.[2] Replacing highly hazardous pesticides such as endosulfan and paraquat with less toxic ones, and training farmers on proper handling of pesticides are expected to reduce acute poisoning. However, despite official adoption of the FAO/WHO International Code of Conduct on the Distribution & Use of Pesticides in 1985, there is evidence from the field that, especially in developing countries, pesticides still pose a serious threat to human health and the environment. Sadly enough, pesticide poisoning also plays today an important role as a mean of suicide.[7]

Exposure to Pesticides

In Europe and North America the focus of concern has generally shifted to chronic effects due to low-level exposures.[8] Farmers and pesticide applicators are particularly prone to adverse effects due to their direct exposure to pesticides at work. In addition, in agricultural areas where pesticides are heavily used, the population nearby is also at risk. Pesticides drift in the air, pollute soil and water resources and can thus contaminate large areas. The widest exposure to pesticides, however, is through residues in food. Exposure is presented as multiple mixtures of chemicals, the toxic effect of which are unknown, particularly over longer time scales.[9] In some cases these substances can interact such that mixtures may have unpredictable and higher toxicities than the individual components themselves.[10] Most research on pesticides is done on the active ingredient. So-called inert ingredients in pesticide formulations that enhance the effect of the active ingredient, however, can also cause substantial health effects.[11] In addition, metabolites of active and inert ingredients can be of even higher toxicity than the original substances.[10]

Fruits and vegetables frequently have the highest levels of pesticide residues—food items that are generally eaten because they are deemed healthy. But also animal products contain pesticide residues that accumulate from feed or from treatment against parasites, or, in the case of fish and seafood, through bioaccumulation in the aquatic food web systems.[12] Studies have shown that people consuming an organic diet may be expected to have consistently lower pesticide intakes than those who consume a conventional diet.[13]

Health Hazards Due to Low-Level, Long-Term Exposure to Pesticides

The literature on health effects of pesticides at general exposure levels is inconclusive, and more research is definitely needed.[14,15] While most industry-financed research suggests that pesticides imply few health risks if they are properly used, there are hundreds of scientific studies published in renowned journals that point out serious health hazards.[10,16] Though there are inherent problems in conducting large-scale experiments and directly assessing causation of these human health problems, the statistical associations between exposure to certain pesticides and the incidence of some diseases are compelling and cannot be ignored.[12] Moreover, some persons have an inherent genetic susceptibility to the health effects of pesticide exposure and are therefore likely to be more at risk than others.

Increased Risk for Cancer and Damage to the Nervous System

There is widespread evidence that exposure to certain pesticides is a significant additional risk factor in many chronic diseases, including different forms of cancer, neurodegenerative diseases and disruptions of the digestive system.[10,12] Various studies among farmers, farm workers and their families showed increased incidences of several types of cancer, such as lymphatic and blood system, lip, stomach, prostate, brain, testes, skin cancers and soft tissue sarcoma.[17,18,14] The International Agency for Research on Cancer recently classified the widely used herbicide glyphosate as probably carcinogenic to humans.[19] Several studies found that exposure to pesticides is statistically associated with an increased risk of developing Parkinson's disease[20,21] and Alzheimer's disease.[22] Whilst aging almost certainly represents the greatest risk factor, low-dose/long-term exposures to pesticides have been implicated as a further factor. Other studies found that chronic low-level exposure to certain pesticides may be related to adverse effects on brain functioning, including changes in attention, speech, sight, memory and emotional aspects.[23,24]

Effects on Immune and Hormone System
There is circumstantial evidence that pesticide exposure is associated with disruption in the immune system,[25] and hormone imbalances.[26,27] These effects may increase the risk for diseases such as obesity and diabetes, autoimmune diseases or reproductive problems. Exposure to certain insecticides may also contribute to the increasing incidence of food allergies in westernized societies.[28] Some studies showed that impacts may be extremely long-term as pesticides can disrupt gene expression and impact the following generations not directly exposed to pesticides.[12]

Effects of Prenatal and Infant Exposure
Unborn and young children are in particular vulnerable to pesticide exposure due to the high rate of growth and complex development processes, the higher dose per body weight and the lower level of detoxifying enzymes compared to adults. Children themselves employed in agricultural work, as often the case particularly in developing countries, are particularly vulnerable to the toxic effects of pesticides. Numerous studies reported for children exposed to high levels of pesticides a delay in their cognitive development, behavioural effects and birth defects.[12,10] A study in California,

US, found that high levels of organophosphorus pesticides in mother's urine were statistically associated with poorer intellectual development and deficits in working memory in the children when they reached 7 years of age.[29] These cognitive effects occurred in children whose mother's urine had levels of organophosphate pesticides that were near the upper end of the range typically found across the general US population. Another study reported that children with higher urinary pesticide levels, mainly from diet, were more likely to be diagnosed with attention deficit/ hyperactivity disorder (ADHD).[30]

Pesticides and the Environment

A large part of the pesticides applied to crops are either taken up by the plants and animals or are degraded by microbial or chemical pathways. A considerable fraction of the amount applied, however, is dispersed into the environment, by air drift, leaching and run-off so that they are found in soils, surface and ground water.[31] Pesticides in freshwater supplies have become a serious and increasingly costly concern, with detected levels often exceeding the set limits (in the EU: 0.1 μg l–1 for any individual active ingredient, or 0.5 μg l–1 for total pesticides). In Switzerland, 70% of surface waters had pesticide levels above the official limit.[32] Pesticides are now found in every habitat on earth and are routinely detected in both marine and terrestrial animals.[33]

Reduced Biodiversity and Ecosystem Services

There is substantial published literature on the effects of pesticides on wildlife and biodiversity. Pesticide use has particularly contributed to the declines in the populations of birds, insects, amphibians and aquatic communities.[34,35,36,37] The effect is either direct through exposure, or indirect through a reduction in food availability. The widespread use of systemic pesticides that are absorbed by the crops is predicted to result in substantial impacts on biodiversity and ecosystem functioning.[38] Studies have shown that systemic insecticides from the group of neonicotinoids can trigger the collapse of bee colonies, thus reducing their function as pollinators.[39] Widespread and continued herbicide application eliminates plant species in fields and bordering areas that provide food and shelter to beneficial insects, spiders and birds. The effects of pesticides are enhanced by loss of habitat due to industrial farming methods.

Aggravated Pest Problems

Pesticide use reduces populations of insects, spiders and birds that naturally control pests. As pests usually recover faster than their predators, pesticide use can aggravate subsequent incidence of pest outbreak. In some cases reduced populations of beneficial insects due to overuse of pesticides contributed to the rise of pests that previously were of minor importance. Cotton and rice are two historical examples of induced pest problems by mismanagement and overuse of insecticides. Another growing concern is that pests and weeds increasingly develop resistance to pesticides. New pesticides are developed or combinations of pesticides are used in order to control them, resulting in additional costs and new side effects.

Economics of Pesticide Use

Pesticide application in agriculture has obvious short-term economic benefits—otherwise farmers would not use them. They may reduce the costs of production (e.g. by using herbicides instead of mechanical weeding) or reduce crop loss due to pest or disease infestation. However, pesticides also cause costs to society in terms of health and environmental costs. These external costs are not (yet) reflected in the market price of pesticides. They include health costs to humans (acute and long-term effects), costs of adverse effects on biodiversity (loss of beneficial insects, pollinators and wildlife), drinking water treatment costs, losses in aquaculture and fisheries, and costs of greenhouse gas emissions during pesticide manufacturing. Due to methodological difficulties and lack of data it is extremely difficult to quantify external costs of pesticide use.

Estimates are in the range of US$4-19 per kg active ingredient, or $19-106 per ha cropland.[1] With some 3.5 billion kg applied worldwide, this would suggest annual costs of $10-60 billion, for a market size of $45 billion.

However, these estimates do not account for the health effects of chronic exposure to pesticides … If only a small fraction of the occurrence of certain diseases like cancer, dementia, diabetes and behavioural disorders can be attributed to pesticides, their external costs would be far higher. In addition, stockpiles of obsolete pesticides exist in many of the least developed countries and are a particularly high risk in situations of political instability. The root causes of the accumulation of these wastes are poor pesticide regulation and management; and over-reliance on chemical pesticides as a first option for pest control. Disposal of obsolete stocks is an extremely expensive undertaking which poses an economic burden on the governments and societies.

Factoring-in Health and Environmental Costs
The question at hand is not to weigh the total benefits of pesticides against their total external costs in order to decide on whether or not to ban them completely—a rather theoretical scenario. More important is to assess to what extent pesticides can be reduced so that the costs of that change (in terms of lower yields or higher production costs) is compensated by an equal reduction in external costs. When health and environmental costs are factored in, pesticide application is only economical at a much lower threshold than what is commonly practiced. In addition, evidence from introducing Integrated Pest Management (IPM) suggests that in a majority of cases pesticides can be reduced through better management practices without substantially reducing yields or increasing costs. The concept of economic thresholds balances the value of crops lost to pests or diseases with the costs of pesticide treatments.

Notes

1. Integrated Pest Management for Sustainable Intensification of Agriculture in Asia and Africa. Pretty, J and Bharucha, ZP. 2015, Insects, pp. Insects 2015, 6, 152-182.

2. IAASTD. International assessment of agricultural knowledge, science and technology for development: global report. Washington DC : Island Press, 2009.

3. Bundesamt für Statistik. Statistik Schweiz. Landwirtschaft Indikatoren. [Online] 24 08 2015. http://www.bfs.admin.ch/bfs/portal/de/index/themen/07/03/blank/ ind24. indicator.240502.2405.html.

4. Fernandez-Cornejo, J, et al. Genetically Engineered Crops in the United States. Washington, DC: United States Department of Agriculture, 2014.

5. Haffmans, S, Sievers-Langer, J and Weber, C. Roundup & Co. Unterschätzte Gefahren. Argumente gegen die Verwendung von Glyphosat und anderen Herbiziden. Hamburg : Agrarkoordination e.V., Pestizid Aktions-Netzwerk e.V., 2014.

6. Williamson, S. Understanding the Full Costs of Pesticides: Experience from the Field, with a Focus on Africa. [book auth.] M. Stoytcheva. Pesticides—The Impacts of Pesticides Exposure. s.l. : InTech, 2011.

7. WHO. Preventing suicide: a global imperative. Geneva : WHO, 2014.

8. Pretty, Jules. The Pesticide Detox—Towards a more sustainable agriculture . London : Earthscan, 2005.

9. Risk assessment of mixtures of pesticides: Current approaches and future strategies. Reffstrup, TK, Larsen, JL and Meyer, O. 2010, Regulatory Toxicology and Pharmacology 56, pp. 174-192.

10. Leu, André. The Myths of Safe Pesticides. Austin, Texas : Acres USA, 2014.

11. Major Pesticides Are More Toxic to Human Cells Than Their Declared Active Principles.Mesnage, R, et al. 2013, BioMed Research International.

12. Greenpeace. Pesticides and Our Health. A Growing Concern. s.l. : Greenpeace UK, 2015.

13. Organic foods: health and environmental advantages and disadvantages. Forman, J, et al. 2012, Pediatrics 130, pp. e1406-e1415.

14. Ntzani, EE, et al. Literature review on epidemiological studies linking exposure to pesticides and health effects. Parma : European Food Safety Authority, 2013.

15. Pesticides and human chronic diseases: evidences, mechanisms, and perspectives. Mostafalou, S and Abdollahi, M. 2013, Toxicology and Applied Pharmacology 268, pp. 157-177.

16. Stoytcheva, M. Pesticides - The Impacts of Pesticides Exposure. s.l. : InTech, 2011.

17. A review of pesticide exposure and cancer incidence in the agricultural health study cohort. Weichenthal, S, Moase, C and Chan, P. 2012, Environmental Health Perspectives 118, pp. 1117-1125.

18. Occupation and cancer—follow-up of 15 million people in five Nordic countries. Pukkala, E, et al. 2009, Acta Oncologica Jan 2009, Vol. 48, No. 5, pp. 646-790.

19. Some Organophosphate Insecticides and Herbicides: Diazinon, Glyphosate, Malathion, Parathion, and Tetrachlorvinphos. IARC. s.l. : IARC, 2015, IARC Monographs on the Evaluation of Carcinogenic Risks to Humans, p. Volume 112.

20. Occupational exposure to pesticides and Parkinson's disease: A systematic review and meta-analysis of cohort studies. Van Maele-Fabry, G, et al. 2012, Environment International 46, pp. 30-43.

21. Is pesticide use related to Parkinson disease? Some clues to heterogeneity in study results. van der Mark, M, et al. 2012, Environmental Health Perspectives 120, pp. 340-7.

22. Linking pesticide exposure and dementia: What is the evidence? Zaganas, I, et al. 2013, Toxicology 307, pp. 3-11.

23. Neurobehavioral performance among agricultural workers and pesticide applicators: a meta-analytic study. Ismail, AA, Bodner, TE and Rohlman, DS. 2012, Occupational Environmental Medicine 69, pp. 475-464.

24. Neurobehavioural problems following low-level exposure to organophosphate pesticides: a systematic and meta-analytic review. Mackenzie, RS, et al. 2013, Critical Reviews in Toxicology 43, pp. 21-44.

25. Pesticide induced immunotoxicity in human: a comprehensive review of the existing evidence. Corsini, E, et al. 2013, Toxicology 307, pp. 123-135.

26. Effect of endocrine disruptor pesticides: A review. Mnif, W, et al. 2011, International Journal of Environmental Research and Public Health 8, pp. 2265-2303.

27. Endocrine disrupters: The hazards for human health. Mandrich, L. 2014, Cloning & Transgenesis 3, p. 1.

28. Dichlorophenol-Containing Pesticides and Allergies: Results from the US National Health and Nutrition Examination Survey 2005–2006. Jerschow, E, et al. 2012, Annals of Allergy, Asthma & Immunology 109, no. 6, pp. 420–25.

29. Prenatal exposure to organophosphate pesticides and IQ in 7-year-old children. Bouchard, MF, et al. 2011, Environmental Health Perspectives 119, pp. 1189-1195.

30. Attention-deficit/hyperactivity disorder and urinary metabolites of organophosphate pesticides. Bouchard, MF, et al. 2010, Pediatrics, 125, pp. e1270-e1277.

31. Vorley, W and Keeney, D. Bugs in the System: Redesigning the Pesticide Industry for Sustainable Agriculture. London : Earthscan, 1998.

32. Pestizidmessungen in Fliessgewässern - schweizweite Auswertung. Munz, N, Leu, C and Wittmer, I. 2012, Aqua & Gas, pp. 32-41.

33. An overview of time trends in organic contaminant concentrations in marine mammals: Going up or down? Law, RJ. 2014, Marine Pollution Bulletin 82, pp. 7-10.

34. Pesticides reduce regional biodiversity of. Beketov, MA, et al. 2013, Proceedings of the National Academy of Sciences USA 110, pp. 11039-11043.

35. A global quantitative synthesis of local and landscape effects on wild bee pollinators in agroecosystems. Kennedy, CM, et al. 2013, Ecology letters 16, pp. 584-599.

36. Declines in insectivorous birds are associated with high neonicotinoid concentrations. Hallman, CA, et al. 2014, Nature, p. 10.1038/nature13531.

37. Ecology: Pesticides linked to bird declines. Goulson, D. 2014, Nature, p. doi: 10.1038/nature13642.

38. Worldwide integrated assessment of the impacts of systemic pesticides on biodiversity and ecosystems. Task Force on Systemic Pesticides. 2015, Environ Science and Pollution Research, pp. 22: 1-154.

39. Sub-lethal exposure to neonicotinoids impaired honey bees winterization before proceeding to colony collapse disorder. Chensheng, L, Warchol, K and Callahan, R. 2014, Bulletin of Insectology 67, pp. 125-130.

> "It's wrong for government to deny us our right to know. Our right to know what is in the food we are buying and our right to choose our preferred food should not be usurped for any reason."

GMOs Should Be Labeled for Transparency

Mark Fergusson

In the following viewpoint, Mark Fergusson argues that consumers have the right to know what is in their food and that the government should deliver transparency with GMO labeling. He claims that because health risks are unknown and reviews are conducted by biased agencies, labeling is essential so that consumers can make their own choices. Fergusson is chief executive officer of Down to Earth Organic & Natural, *a community-based business of health food stores in Hawaii dedicated to promoting healthy living, respect for the environment, and sustainable organic farming.*

As you read, consider the following questions:

1. According to the viewpoint, why are the limited risk assessments conducted to date poor predictors of the long-term safety of GMOs?
2. According to the viewpoint, what is problematic about the regulatory reviews conducted by government agencies?
3. According to the viewpoint, why is it important to consumers to have GMO labeling?

One of the most dangerous and least understood experiments with human health the world has ever known is currently underway without your consent—in your household and households across the nation, indeed throughout our entire planet. It is the wholesale contamination of the world's food supply with genetically modified organisms (GMOs).

A GMO is the result of a laboratory process where genes are taken from one species and inserted into another in an attempt to obtain a desired trait or characteristic. GMOs are also known as genetically engineered-, bio-engineered-, biotech crops, or transgenic organisms.

While GMO proponents say their goal is to increase nutritional benefits or productivity, the two main traits that have been added to date are herbicide tolerance and the ability of the plant to produce its own pesticide. These results have no health benefits, only economic benefits to the companies that produce them, at the cost of significant negative consequences.

Introduced in 1996, the genetic engineering of plants and animals today looms as one of the greatest and most intractable environmental and health challenges of the 21st Century. With promises of making more and supposedly "better" food, this new technology has invaded our farmlands, grocery stores, and our kitchen pantries by fundamentally altering some of our most important staple food crops.

Most Food on Supermarket Shelves Is Contaminated by GMOs!

As of 2011, 88% of US corn is genetically engineered as are 94% of soy, 95% of sugar beets, 90% of canola oil, 90% of cotton, and about 80% of Hawaiian papaya. Also, this spring marked the first planting of GMO alfalfa.[1,2] In 2003 the Grocery Manufacturers Association estimated that GMOs were present in 70% to 75% of conventional processed food on supermarket shelves.[3] That number must be even higher today. Everything including bread, cereal, frozen pizza, soup, soda—all sorts of processed foods—now contain genetically engineered ingredients. Another common source of GMO food is dairy products from cows injected with the genetically modified hormone Recombinant Bovine Growth Hormone (rBGH).

Because there are no laws mandating that these ingredients must be labeled as genetically modified, consumers are most likely unknowingly consuming genetically modified ingredients.

Are GMOs Safe to Eat?

One of the most common concerns about the prevalence of GMOs in North America is whether they are safe for human consumption. The sad truth is many of the foods that are most popular with children contain GMOs. Cereals, snack bars, snack boxes, cookies, processed lunch meats, and crackers all contain large amounts of high-risk food ingredients.

While many in the scientific community assert that GMO foods are not toxic and are safe, a significant number of scientists are sounding the alarm. They say genetic engineering poses risks that scientists simply do not know enough to identify. In fact, based on what little is known about GMOs, many scientists have identified a variety of ways in which genetically engineered organisms could adversely impact both human health and the environment.

Health Risks Are Unknown

Specific engineered organisms may be harmful by virtue of the novel gene combinations they possess. No one knows with certainty how these new life forms will behave in the future, so the limited risk assessments conducted to date are poor predictors of the safety of GMOs over the long term.

Risk assessment is further challenged by the highly complex web of regulatory review, which involves three government agencies and dozens of departments with competing interests that render government oversight practically toothless.

At the most basic level, so-called government risk assessment is suspect because it actually conducts no research on its own. Health and safety reviews rely almost entirely on data supplied by the very companies seeking approvals for their new GMO products. This is a serious conflict of interest that brings into question the validity of safety assurances from the government.

Government Wrongly Says GMO Labeling Not Needed

Government and the GMO industry say these new crops are environmentally safe and that there's no nutritional difference between GMOs and conventional crops. According to them we don't need to know, so no labeling is required.

Therefore, since their commercialization in 1992, the US Food and Drug Administration (FDA) has rejected labeling of GMO foods. By contrast, labeling is required in countries including the 27 member nations of the European Union, Australia, New Zealand, Japan, Korea, Brazil and China. Currently pending before the (FDA) is a decision on whether to approve the first genetically engineered animal—a salmon that grows to maturity twice as fast as normal and, if approved, whether to require labeling on this salmon.

Consumers Want Right to Choose

Down to Earth joins the call for GMO labeling so that, if we want, we can choose not to eat GMOs. The general public agrees.

A 2003 poll by ABC news showed that, "… huge majorities of Americans favor mandatory labeling—92 percent for genetically modified foods, and 85 percent for food from farm animals that have been fed hormones or antibiotics."[4]

These figures track with Hawaii residents' preferences who, in a 2007 UH survey, indicated that they want choice. "…More than 90 percent of those surveyed supported the labeling of GM foods, 68 percent indicated that such labeling was needed, and 50 percent felt that not labeling GM food products was a violation of the consumer's rights."[5]

The simple truth is that most people want the right to choose what they eat and what they feed their families. For consumers to make informed decisions, the public deserves a truthful marketplace.

Look for the Organic or Non-GMO Project Verified Seal

One of the ways to avoid GMOs is to choose foods that have the Organic seal, which certifies that GMOs were not used in production.

Another option is to look for the Non-GMO Project Verified Seal issued by the Non-GMO Project.[6]

Down to Earth, along with the natural products industry, strongly supports this Project. It is a non-profit collaboration of companies, farmers, and consumers offering North America's first program that verifies non-GMO products. The Non-GMO Project provides a seal of approval to manufacturers that meet their rigorous non-GMO standards. Backed by independent testing, the "Non-GMO Project Verified" seal means that GMO contamination has been avoided throughout the growth and harvesting of crops, their processing, storage and packaging. Over 3,000 products have been verified to date, with thousands more in the process.

As manufacturers begin to include the "Non-GMO Project Verified" logo on their packaging, you will see more and more of the verified products on our shelves. Consumers have the right to choose what foods to eat and feed their families. This Non-GMO logo enables consumers to exercise this right! We get to exercise this right only with products from manufacturers that voluntarily comply with the Non-GMO Project's standards. In contrast, GMO labeling should be required on all food packaging.

GMO Labeling Is Key to Our Right to Know!

Few choices in our daily lives are as important as the food choices we make for ourselves and our families. We should be the ones in control, not government. It's wrong for government to deny us our right to know. Our right to know what is in the food we are buying and our right to choose our preferred food should not be usurped for any reason.

Most Hawaii residents want GMO labeling and many are not convinced that GMOs are safe. Some oppose them based on scientific studies; others oppose them on religious, spiritual, philosophical, or ethical beliefs. While we have different reasons for wanting to know what is in our food, the one thing no one should deny is our right to know.

Down to Earth calls on Congress to support labeling of foods that contain GMOs.

Notes

1. USDA Economic Research Service, "Adoption of Genetically Engineered Crops in the US (link is external)."

2. GMO Compass, "USA: In 2010, more genetically modified crops once again," June 30, 2010 (Accessed 12-9-11).

3. US Food and Drug Administration, FDA Consumer Magazine, "Genetic Engineering: The Future of Foods," Nov-Dec 2003 http://permanent.access.gpo.gov/lps1609/www.fda.gov/fdac/features/2003/6... (link is external) (Accessed 12-9-11).

4. ABC News, "Poll: Modified Foods Give Consumers Pause," July 15, 2003 http://abcnews.go.com/Business/story?id=86497&page=1 (link is external) (Accessed 12-12-11).

5. Univ. of Hawaii-Manoa, Cooperative Extension Service, "Attitudes of Hawai'i Consumers Toward Genetically Modified Fruit," http://scholarspace.manoa.hawaii.edu/bitstream/handle/10125/12173/BIO-7.... (link is external) (Accesses 12-12-11).

6. The Non-GMO Project, https://www.nongmoproject.org/ (link is external) (Accessed 12-9-11).

> *"Failure to provide qualifying or explanatory information can also run the risk that a process label can stigmatize conventional products."*

Labeling GMOs May Create Misleading Stigma

Steve Armstrong

In the following viewpoint, excerpted for length, Steve Armstrong argues that process labeling is not a straightforward matter of transparency and that irresponsible labeling can mislead consumers instead. He makes note of the problematic inferences that can arise from claims unaccompanied by sufficient disclosures and urges marketers to exercise critical thought and caution if they choose to label products. Armstrong is an independent advisor on food law and regulation for EAS Consulting Group. He has over 20 years of experience counseling companies on marketing and regulatory matters and is a member of the Board of Directors of the Food and Drug Law Institute.

As you read, consider the following questions:

1. What can consumers' interest in process labeling be attributed to?
2. In what ways can labeling confuse or mislead consumers?
3. Why does the FDA not require GMO labeling?

"Process Labeling: The Challenges of Transparency," with permission from Food and Drug Law Institute," by Steve Armstrong.

I t's nearly impossible these days to do grocery shopping without running into a label that says something about how a food was made, where it came from or, more often than not, what kinds of things were not done to the food. Claims about how food was grown, produced, prepared and packaged—and, in particular how the earth and its inhabitants were treated along the way—have cropped up in nearly every aisle in the supermarket. It's hard to avoid "fair trade" coffee, "cage-free" eggs, "rBST-free" milk, or "Non-GMO" orange juice, not to mention products claiming to be "natural" or "organic." Process labeling is coming to predominate our food marketing, quite often taking precedence over more traditional food attributes. To take but one example, the principal display panel of a current meat product proclaims that it is "100% grass fed," "free range," "all natural," "minimally processed" and with no antibiotics or added hormones. Crowded tight with all these claims, the front panel says nothing about the attributes that have long been held to define food—taste, aroma, and nutrition.[1] Given the increasing popularity of process labeling, it is essential for marketers and their advisors to understand the challenges of making these claims and the legal standards that apply to them. While such claims may seem attractive to food companies seeking a competitive advantage or greater transparency, it can prove challenging to ensure that they are truthful, non-misleading, and adequately substantiated. Success requires a sound scientific basis for the claim, strict supply chain oversight and control, and clear, direct, and properly qualified language in labeling. Anyone undertaking these challenges should understand clearly why process labeling claims are so popular. It's also necessary to understand how the misbranding and deception principles of the Federal Food, Drug, and Cosmetic Act (FDCA)[2] and the Federal Trade Commission Act (FTC Act), including the FTC's Policy Statement on Deception (Deception Policy) and its Guides for the Use of Environmental Marketing Claims (Green Guides)[3] can help chart the path toward diligent compliance and consumer satisfaction.

Rise in Popularity

Mounting evidence of the popularity of process labeling claims can readily be seen in the United States and markets around the world. For one thing, consumer purchases of organic foods have reached record levels, amounting to over $43 billion last year, and up 11% over the previous year.[4] In addition, the market for "eco" labels is robust, with the Eco Label Index listing more than 460 labels in use in nearly 200 countries, covering 25 industry sectors.[5] A recent survey of consumers conducted by the US Farmers and Ranchers Alliance found that 70 percent said their purchasing decisions were affected by how food was grown and raised, and three-quarters said they think about these issues while grocery shopping.[6] Food companies are embracing process labeling in the name of "transparency" with many committing to providing more information via labeling about how food is produced.[7]

A study published in 2015 by the nonprofit Council on Agriculture Science and Technology (CAST) helps explain the phenomenon.[8] Because much of our food comes to us from a global supply chain, the study said, we as consumers have little opportunity to see production processes directly or know much about them. This fact can give rise to worries and concerns about how food is made and whether best practices are always followed. The study attributed interest in process labeling to "desires for individual control and a diffuse distrust in the safety and health of food produced by modern agriculture."[9] Other observers have said that, ironically, the industry's success in putting safe, nourishing, and relatively inexpensive food on the tables of Americans has fueled the interest in food production and calls for transparency:

> As top concerns for consumers are already largely being met, there is a freedom that was not historically available to delve deeper into food issues, to ponder how food was grown and raised and to think about these matters while checking out. Consumers are not wrong for doing this; it is the fundamental right of the consumer to question.[10]

When viewed in the context of dramatic advances in food production, coupled with emerging consumer concerns over safety, health, and the environment, "it should not be surprising that some consumers are demanding more information—via labeling—about how their food is produced."[11]

The Case for—and Against—Process Labels

The process-labeling phenomenon presents an opportunity for a food company seeking greater transparency with consumers. The CAST study found that process labels "can effectively bridge the informational gap between producers and consumers, satisfy consumer demand for broader and more stringent quality assurance criteria, and ultimately create value for both consumers and producers."[12] In particular, process labeling can help a food company aspiring toward transparency convince consumers that its values align with theirs.

Unfortunately, a process labeling claim is often presented without any qualification or other information that could help explain how it fits into a transparency mission. This is, no doubt, because many process-related issues are complex and difficult to execute. Providing information sufficient to explain an issue can take up valuable labeling space and risk losing those with short attention spans. On the other hand, truncated communications can alienate, confuse, or even mislead concerned consumers.

Consider the label of a current canned tuna claiming prominently to be "sustainable." The terms "pole" and "troll-caught" appear next to the claim. On a side panel, one sees dolphin and turtle logos and "FADs" circled in red and crossed out. No explanation accompanies the fishing terms, the logos, or the acronym. However, an Internet search can reveal that the acronym stands for "Fish Aggregating Device," a controversial method of commercial, deep-sea fishing using long, cylindrical nets that float unattended across the oceans and can presumably snare dolphins, turtles, and just about anything that swims by. Yet the label does not say whether the product avoids FADs altogether or why the alternate methods are preferable, much less their impact on dolphins, turtles, and other sea creatures.

In addition to leaving consumers confused, failure to provide qualifying or explanatory information can also run the risk that a process label—particularly one about a process that is avoided—can stigmatize conventional products. The authors of the CAST study found that process labels frequently leave that kind of impression "because the [process] label portrays the conventional product in an implicitly negative way."[13] The authors saw a particular danger here:

> This type of stigmatization of the conventional product can be particularly problematic in situations in which no scientific evidence exists that the food produced with the conventional process causes harm, or even that it is compositionally any different.[14]

The potentially unintended and undesirable consequences include increasing food prices, introducing unwarranted quality or health expectations and, in the end, "stunting scientific and technological advances in agriculture."[15] Indeed, FDA has long advised that "Non-GMO" claims should not suggest that a food is safer or more nutritious simply because it avoided the use of genetic engineering.[16] Still, "Non-GMO" continues to be a popular claim, often appearing without any information why consumers should care that their food was made without ingredients derived from genetic engineering.

The right amount of explanatory information on the label or an accompanying website can address these issues. While it may not be possible to explain all the environmental benefits of certain fishing practices on the label of a five-ounce can of tuna, there surely is enough space for "Learn about our sustainable fishing practices," accompanied by a URL for a website discussing the issue in greater detail. Further, where the non-use of GMOs does not result in a food that is materially different, that fact should be disclosed in the labeling, along with a reassurance that FDA regards GMO foods as safe for consumption.

The Questions for Marketers

While process labeling can effectively respond to consumers wanting a stronger connection to their food, it's necessary, in the first instance, to determine what issues are relevant to consumers, just how much information they want and how much is necessary to ensure that the communication, in context, is truthful and non-misleading. Balancing these competing objectives is not easy. At a minimum, process claims such as "Non-GMO" or "no FADs," should include enough information to make clear what the process-related attribute delivers—and what it doesn't.

Answers to these questions can begin to emerge when considering the labeling requirements of the FDCA and the deception safeguards set forth in the FTC Act, as interpreted by the FTC's Deception Policy and Green Guides. The core provisions of these laws and policies have special relevance to process labeling claims and can provide the framework for a thorough and well-grounded analysis.

[...]

Communication Challenges

For process labeling claims, it's hard to overstate the importance of the first step in the analysis—identifying all the messages, both explicit and implicit, that are reasonably conveyed by the labeling or advertising in the context in which the claim is presented. This is especially important, because process labeling claims can be highly inferential, i.e., they are capable of sending a great variety of implied messages and reassurances. While some may be accurate, others may be quite off the mark.

Problematic inferences can arise simply by virtue of the position that the process claim occupies on the label in relation to other labeling elements or the failure to provide an adequate disclosure about what the claim does and doesn't mean for the average consumer. A process claim presented prominently on the front panel—e.g., "natural," "organic," or "non-GMO"—in the company of equally prominent nutrition, health, or wellness messages, can leave consumers with a powerful impression that the touted process has helped make the food safer or healthier, when, as often as not, the process has done nothing of the sort. And silence, i.e., the failure to offer any qualification, explanation or disclaimer, can leave much room for the reasonable consumer to imagine benefits where none exist.

Case Studies

Claims about a food's non-use of GMOs, which can readily mislead consumers unless accompanied by adequate disclosures, are a case in point. A recent survey concluded that an overwhelming majority of consumers worldwide think non-GMO foods are healthier than foods made with GMOs.[26] However, FDA has found no scientific basis to require GMO labeling because the scientific consensus—announced not only by FDA but at least a half- dozen other respected scientific organizations—is that GMO foods are safe and not materially different from non-GMO foods.[27]

Now, in light of these facts, consider the label of a popular granola bar, covered with attractive claims—"100% whole grains" that are "super," "healthy" and "gluten free"—and which also shows the following statements prominently, right alongside each other on the principal display panel:

HEALTHY

NON-GMO

Does this placement imply that non-GMO foods are healthier than their conventional competitors? Or at least create an ambiguity? Is it a reasonable understanding? At any rate, the label does not disclose the scientific consensus that GMOs are safe and that avoiding them does not bring a health benefit. No information reflecting that consensus is provided, leaving a reasonable consumer with the mistaken impression that the avoidance of GMOs might indeed contribute to good health. The inference could have been avoided if the label had noted FDA's position on the same panel, or at least on an adjoining one, an approach that is strongly suggested by the Green Guides.[28] An effective disclaimer could have stated simply, "Foods that avoid using GMOs are not healthier than GMO foods. FDA considers GMO crops to be safe." A link to FDA's policies on bioengineering and GMO labeling would have helped reinforce the message.

Disclosures and disclaimers can provide information necessary for a consumer to understand a process labeling claim and consider whether it has any significance from a health, safety, or environmental perspective. When no meaningful difference exists, or where the benefit of the process is negligible, it's important to convey that information.[29] The Green Guides require that disclosures be "clear and prominent," in plain language, and placed in close proximity to the claim.[30] This means that where the claim is made on the principal display panel, the disclaimer belongs there as well. For example, milk containers will sometimes advertise their non-use of rBST, but at the insistence of some state regulators, such labels make clear, on the same panel, that the practice does not result in milk that is significantly different from milk that has not undergone the rBST removal process.

Officials at USDA's Food Safety and Inspection Service (FSIS) who review the labels of meat and poultry products before they are released into the market, routinely allow certain process claims, but only with the appropriate disclaimers appearing immediately next to the claims. For example, a pork product claiming to be raised without antibiotics must include the disclaimer, "Federal Regulations Prohibit the Use of Hormones in Pork" directly next to or underneath the claim. A promise of "no nitrites or nitrates added" must also specify, next to the claim, the ingredients in which nitrites and nitrates occur naturally. USDA also permits qualifying products to claim that they are "natural," but requires the following explanation next to the claim: "No artificial ingredients / Minimally processed."

Marketers and their advisors must consider process labeling communications carefully and with a clear eye to what is and is not being conveyed to the reasonable consumer, both directly and by implication. Only then can it be determined what information needs to be included so that the consumer understands the claim and its significance in clear and unambiguous terms. This is not an easy task, and, of course, the job of ensuring that the claim is supported by adequate technical and scientific data brings challenges of its own.

[…]

Conclusion

Process labeling claims must be used thoughtfully, and with careful attention paid to context, consumer perception, and messaging. It is essential to think critically about all the messages that the labeling elements and their relative placement may reasonably convey and structure the communication to ensure that the consumer understands the significance of the claim. Disclosures necessary to avoid any unsupported messages must be provided, since a process by itself may not necessarily promote wellness or safety, or even produce a material difference. Processes and systems that can support the claim have to be established and monitored on a continuing basis.

In the end, marketers and their advisors will likely find that process labeling is worth the effort because it can connect a product with the core values of consumers who want the products they buy to say something about who they are—or who they might wish to be. But execution is neither simple nor straightforward. It's a project that requires honesty, care, and hard work.

Notes

1. Nutrilab, Inc. v. Schweiker, 713 F.2d 335 (7th Cir. 1983), discussing Federal Food, Drug, and Cosmetic Act § 201(g)(1)(C), 21 U.S.C. § 321(g)(1)(C).

2. Federal Food, Drug, and Cosmetic Act, §§ 201, 403; 21 U.S.C. § 321, 343.

3. Federal Trade Commission Act §§ 5, 12-15; 15 U.S.C. §§ 45, 52-55; FTC Policy Statement on Deception, October 11, 1983, Appended to Cliffdale Associates, Inc., 103 F.T.C. 110, 174 (1984) https://www.ftc.gov/system/files/documents/public_statements/410531/831014deceptionstmt.pdf; Guide to Environmental Marketing Claims, 16 C.F.R., Part 260, https://www.ftc.gov/enforcement/rules/rulemaking-regulatory-reform-proceedings/green-guides.

4. "US Organic Sales Post New Record," Organic Trade Association, May 16, 2016 (See https://www.ota.com/news/press-releases/19031).

5. http://www.ecolabelindex.com.

6. http://www.cattlenetwork.com/news/industry/us-farmers-and-ranchers-alliance-survey-reveals-consumers-attitudes-sustainability-and.

7. See, e.g., "Consumers Demand Transparency in the Food Industry," Prepared Foods, January 24, 2017 (see http://www.preparedfoods.com/articles/119315-consumers-demand-transparency-in-the-food-industry); "Food Companies on the Front Line of a Transparency Revolution," Center for Food Integrity, September 15, 2016 (see http://www.foodintegrity.org/blog/2016/09/15/food-companies-on-the-front-line-of-a-transparency-revolution); "Campbell Labels Will Disclose GMO Ingredients," New York Times Business Day, January 7, 2016 (See https://www.nytimes.com/2016/01/08/business/campbell-labels-will-disclose-gmo-ingredients.html?_r=0).

8. "Process Labeling of Food: Consumer Behavior, the Agricultural Sector, and Policy Recommendations," Issue Paper No. 56, Council for Agricultural Science and Technology, October 2015 (Available for download at https://www.cast-science.org/download. cfm?PublicationID=283819&File=10306205e87081c6f250782a2f3b38423751TR).

9. CAST Issue Paper No. 56, at p. 1.

10. The Communication Scarcity in Agriculture, J. Eise, W. Hode (New York, N.Y. 2017), at p. 46.

11. Id.

12. Cast Issue Paper No. 56, at p. 1.

13. Id. at p. 12.

14. Id. at p. 1.

15. Id. at p. 2.

16. "Guidance for Industry: Voluntary Labeling Indicating Whether Foods Have or Have Not Been Derived from Genetically Engineered Plants," November 2015, at Section III.B (see https://www.fda.gov/RegulatoryInformation/Guidances/ucm059098.htm).

26. "87% of Consumers Globally Think Non-GMO is 'Healthier,' But Where's the Evidence?" E. Watson, Food Navigator, August 13, 2015 (see http://www.foodnavigator-usa.com/Manufacturers/87-of-consumers-globally-think-non-GMO-is-healthier).

27. Id., and "Statement of Policy—Foods Derived from New Plant Varieties," FDA, Federal Register, Volume 57, May 29, 1992 at Section V (see https://www.fda.gov/Food/GuidanceRegulation/GuidanceDocumentsRegulatoryInformation/Biotechnology/ucm096095.htm).

28. Green Guides, 16 C.F.R. § 260.3(a).

29. The CAST study strongly recommended that process labels claiming a product is "free of" a certain production related process should disclose the current scientific consensus regarding the importance (or non-importance) of that attribute. CAST Issue Paper No. 56, at p. 13.

> *"Without such testing, and full access to industry data, the FDA cannot credibly decree, declare or certify that GMOs are safe."*

There Is Insufficient Safety Testing for GMOs

Gary Ruskin

In the following viewpoint, Gary Ruskin argues that because the FDA does not conduct its own safety testing on GMOs and relies on self-reported data from agrichemical corporations, the existing testing regime for GMOs is insufficient. Raising concerns of fraudulent or intentionally omitted studies, Ruskin claims that the FDA cannot substantiate its claim that GMOs are safe. Ruskin is co-director of US Right to Know, a non-profit organization that works for transparency and accountability in the US food system. Ruskin has been working on food issues since 1998.

As you read, consider the following questions:

1. What is the FDA's rationale for not conducting its own direct tests on whether GE foods are safe?
2. Why is most animal safety testing insufficient?
3. Why should the FDA not trust the self-reported studies of the agrichemical industry?

In recent testimony before Congress, the FDA stated that it is "confident that the GE foods in the US marketplace today are as safe as their conventional counterparts."[1]

However, FDA does not itself test whether genetically engineered foods are safe. The FDA has repeatedly made this clear. As Jason Dietz, a policy analyst at FDA explains about genetically engineered food: "It's the manufacturer's responsibility to insure that the product is safe."[2] Or, as FDA spokesperson Theresa Eisenman said, "it is the manufacturer's responsibility to ensure that the [GMO] food products it offers for sale are safe…"[3]

Nor does the FDA require independent pre-market safety testing for genetically engineered food. As a matter of practice, the agrichemical companies submit their own studies to the FDA as part of a voluntary "consultation." Moreover, the FDA does not require the companies to submit full and complete information about these studies. Rather, as the FDA has testified, "After the studies are completed, a summary of the data and information on the safety and nutritional assessment are provided to the FDA for review."[4]

That the FDA does not see the complete data and studies is a problem, according to a *Biotechnology and Genetic Engineering Reviews* article by William Freese and David Schubert:

> the FDA never sees the methodological details, but rather only limited data and the conclusions the company has drawn from its own research … the FDA does not require the submission of data. And, in fact, companies have failed to comply with FDA requests for data beyond that which they submitted initially. Without test protocols or other important data, the FDA is unable to identify unintentional mistakes, errors in data interpretation, or intentional deception…[5]

At the end of the consultation, the FDA issues a letter ending the consultation. Here is a typical response from FDA, in its letter to Monsanto about its MON 810 Bt corn:

> Based on the safety and nutritional assessment you have conducted, it is our understanding that Monsanto has concluded

that corn products derived from this new variety are not materially different in composition, safety, and other relevant parameters from corn currently on the market, and that the genetically modified corn does not raise issues that would require premarket review or approval by FDA … as you are aware, **it is Monsanto's responsibility to ensure that foods marketed by the firm are safe, wholesome** [emphasis ours] and in compliance with all applicable legal and regulatory requirements.[6]

This testing regime is insufficient for several other reasons. Most of the animal safety testing prepared for the FDA is merely short-term. A study in the International Journal of Biological Sciences summarizes the typical testing regime: "The most detailed regulatory tests on the GMOs are three-month long feeding trials of laboratory rats, which are biochemically assessed." Such tests may well be too brief in duration to uncover pathologies that develop more slowly, such as many types of organ damage, endocrine disturbances and cancer.[7]

There are too few peer-reviewed studies on the health risks of genetically engineered food. In their 2004 article in *Biotechnology and Genetic Engineering Reviews,* William Freese and David Schubert wrote that, "Published, peer-reviewed studies, particularly in the area of potential human health impacts, are rare. For instance, the EPA's human health assessment of Bt crops cites 22 unpublished corporate studies, with initially only one ancillary literature citation."[8] Similarly, a 2014 review in Environment International of 21 studies of the effects of genetically engineered foods on the digestive tracts of rats found an "incomplete picture" regarding "the toxicity (and safety) of GM products consumed by humans and animals."[9] In other words, it concludes that there is not enough evidence to say that genetically engineered foods are safe to eat.

The FDA permits companies to submit their own safety studies, but does not require independent ones. However, the evidence regarding pharmaceutical studies strongly suggests that industry-funded studies are more likely than independent ones to be favorable to industry. Here's Ben Goldacre's review of this evidence:

in 2010, three researchers from Harvard and Toronto found all the trials looking at five major classes of drug—antidepressants, ulcer drugs and so on—then measured two key features: were they positive, and were they funded by industry? They found over five hundred trials in total: 85 per cent of the industry-funded studies were positive, but only 50 per cent of the government funded trials were. That's a very significant difference.

In 2007, researchers looked at every published trial that set out to explore the benefit of a statin ... This study found 192 trials in total, either comparing one statin against another, or comparing a statin against a different kind of treatment. Once the researchers controlled for other factors ... they found that industry-funded trials were twenty times more likely to give results favoring the test drug. Again, that's a very big difference.

We'll do one more. In 2006, researchers looked into every trial of psychiatric drugs in four academic journals over a ten-year period, finding 542 trial outcomes in total. Industry sponsors got favorable outcomes for their own drug 78 per cent of the time, while independently funded trials only gave a positive result in 48 per cent of cases.[10]

These results present a compelling argument for FDA to require independent pre-market safety testing for genetically engineered food, but the FDA fails to do so.

Perhaps more importantly, the agrichemical industry is under no obligation to report the results of all their studies. How do we know that they are not suppressing evidence of health risks of genetically engineered food? It is well-known that in other industries "publication bias" and the suppression of studies is commonplace. That is certainly true in the pharmaceutical industry. Here, for example, is Ben Goldacre's description of missing evidence in trials on antidepressants:

> researchers found seventy-four studies in total, representing 12,500 patients' worth of data. Thirty-eight of these trials had positive results, and found that the new drug worked; thirty-six were negative. The results were therefore an even split between success and failure for the drugs, in reality. Then the researchers

set about looking for these trials in the published academic literature, the material available to doctors and patients. This provided a very different picture. Thirty-seven of the positive trials—all but one—were published in full, often with much fanfare. But the trials with negative results had a very different fate: only three were published. Twenty-two were simply lost to history, never appearing anywhere other than in those dusty, disorganized, thin FDA files. The remaining eleven which had negative results in the FDA summaries did appear in the academic literature, but were written up as if the drug was a success ...

This was a remarkable piece of work, spread over twelve drugs from all the major manufacturers, with no stand-out bad guy. It very clearly exposed a broken system: in reality we have thirty-eight positive trials and thirty-seven negative ones; in the academic literature we have forty-eight positive trials and three negative ones.[11]

Why shouldn't we expect the agrichemical industry to follow the pharmaceutical industry's pattern of suppressing negative results? This question seems especially relevant, given the agrichemical industry's history of suppressing evidence of health risks of their other products and operations. It makes no sense for the FDA to trust an industry with such a record.

It is also worth remembering that in the US there is a history of fraud in toxicological testing. As Dan Fagin and Marianne Lavelle explain in their book *Toxic Deception,* "The US regulatory system for chemical products is tailor-made for fraud. The subjects are arcane, the results subjective, the regulators overmatched, and the real work conducted by—or for—the manufacturers themselves."[12] Regarding Monsanto's role in such frauds, they write that:

Paul Wright had been a research chemist at Monsanto before he went to work for IBT [then the nation's largest toxicology lab] in 1971 as its chief rat toxicologist. Wright stayed at the lab for only 18 months before he returned to Monsanto ... But it was long enough, the [federal] government investigators concluded, for him to be in the middle of a series of apparently fraudulent studies that benefitted Monsanto products … In all three cases [regarding an herbicide and a chlorinator], the [federal government] investigators wrote in an internal memo, there was evidence that Monsanto executives knew that the studies were faked but sent them to the FDA and the EPA anyway.[13]

Finally, how can we assess the health risks of genetically engineered foods that are currently on the market? At this time, we can't. The FDA does not require any post-market studies of health risks of genetically engineered food. As a 2010 study in the *International Journal of Biological Sciences* points out, "although some stakeholders claim that a history of safe use of GMOs can be upheld, there are no human or animal epidemiological studies to support such a claim as yet, in particular because of the lack of labeling and traceability in GMO-producing countries."[14] Without such epidemiological studies on genetically engineered food, we can't know whether GMOs are safe or not, and if they cause illnesses, what they are, who is afflicted, and with what frequency.

Perhaps not coincidentally, there is a similar problem with testing of pesticide levels on the fruits and vegetables eaten by American consumers. A November 2014 report by the US Government Accountability Office found that the FDA only tests the pesticide levels of less than one per thousand imported fruits and vegetables, and one per hundred of those grown domestically. GAO concluded that the FDA's testing program is not "statistically valid."[15] *The Washington Post* explains the GAO's conclusion: "The US Food and Drug Administration does not perform enough pesticide residue tests—on either imported or domestic foods—to say whether the American food supply is safe …"[16]

Of course, the agrichemical companies say their genetically engineered foods are safe. What's curious about this is that they have enough money to carry out independent pre-market and post-market testing of the health risks of their products. Such testing would be an easy way to put to rest any questions about health risks. But they don't. Why not? Also, the agrichemical industry could lobby for federal laws or rules requiring pre-market and post-market safety testing for genetically engineered foods. And they would likely prevail. They haven't done that either. Why not? It suggests they don't want to know the answers, or they don't want us to know the answers. Or both. This doesn't inspire trust.

Even at the outset, some FDA scientists had concerns about the health risks of genetically engineered food. According to the *New York Times*,

> Among them was Dr. Louis J. Pribyl, one of 17 government scientists working on a policy for genetically engineered food. Dr. Pribyl knew from studies that toxins could be unintentionally created when new genes were introduced into a plant's cells. But under the new edict, the government was dismissing that risk and any other possible risk as no different from those of conventionally derived food. That meant biotechnology companies would not need government approval to sell the foods they were developing.
>
> "This is the industry's pet idea, namely that there are no unintended effects that will raise the F.D.A.'s level of concern," Dr. Pribyl wrote in a fiery memo to the F.D.A. scientist overseeing the policy's development. "But time and time again, there is no data to back up their contention."
>
> Dr. Pribyl, a microbiologist, was not alone at the agency. Dr. Gerald Guest, director of the center of veterinary medicine, wrote that he and other scientists at the center had concluded there was "ample scientific justification" to require tests and a government review of each genetically engineered food before it was sold.
>
> Three toxicologists wrote, "The possibility of unexpected, accidental changes in genetically engineered plants justifies a limited traditional toxicological study."[17]

The federal government's premise for lax regulation of GMOs was the notion of "substantial equivalence"—that new genetically engineered foods were substantially equivalent to regular foods, so there was no need for regulation. As the FDA's 1992 "guidance to industry" stated, "FDA believes that the new techniques are extensions at the molecular level of traditional methods and will be used to achieve the same goals as pursued with traditional plant breeding."[18] It was with this idea that the agrichemical industry evaded rigorous safety testing.

But the premise of "substantial equivalence" was dubious from the start. It was an a priori political concept—adopted without studies or evidence—to treat genetically engineered food as GRAS (Generally Regarded As Safe). It was claimed by the agrichemical industry, not proven by independent study. For this reason, some FDA staff opposed the idea of "substantial equivalence." For example, Dr. Linda Kahl, an FDA compliance officer, was concerned about unpredictable or unknown safety risks from genetically engineered food. She wrote:

> The process of genetic engineering and traditional breeding are different, and according to the technical experts in the agency, they lead to different risks," Dr. Kahl wrote. "There is no data that addresses the relative magnitude of risk—for all we know, the risks may be lower for genetically engineered foods than for foods produced by traditional breeding. But the acknowledgment that the risks are different is lost in the attempt to hold to the doctrine that the product and not the process is regulated.[19]

Along the same lines, E. J. Matthews of the FDA's Toxicology Group warned that "genetically modified plants could ... contain unexpected high concentrations of plant toxicants" and that these could be "uniquely different chemicals that are usually expressed in unrelated plants."[20]

"Substantial equivalence is a pseudo-scientific concept," explained a commentary by Erik Millstone, Eric Brunner and Sue Mayer in *Nature,* "because it is a commercial and political judgment masquerading as if it were scientific. It is, moreover, inherently anti-scientific because it was created primarily to provide an excuse for not requiring biochemical or toxicological tests."[21]

As Consumers Union senior staff scientist Michael Hansen points out, even the FDA itself has explicitly rejected its own premise of "substantial equivalence." It did so in its 2001 proposed rule on pre-market notice of genetically engineered food. The FDA wrote:

> Because some rDNA-induced unintended changes are specific to a transformational event (e.g., those resulting from insertional

mutagenesis), FDA believes that it needs to be provided with information about foods from all separate transformational events, even when the agency has been provided with information about foods from rDNA-modified plants with the same intended new trait and has had no questions about such foods … In contrast, the agency does not believe that it needs to receive information about foods from plants derived through narrow crosses [such as traditional plant breeding][22]

Yet, even though the FDA has acknowledged the flaws in its own premise of "substantial equivalence," the underlying policy lives on—now without any justification at all.

So, the FDA states that it is "confident" about the safety of GMOs currently in the marketplace. But it does not itself conduct safety testing on GMOs. It does not sponsor independent safety testing. It does not require independent safety testing. It does not require long-term safety testing, to uncover ill effects that have delayed onset. It does not have access to the full data and content of all industry safety testing. And it does not require post-market epidemiological testing. Without such testing, and full access to industry data, the FDA cannot credibly decree, declare or certify that GMOs are safe.

Notes

1. Statement of Michael M. Landa, J.D., Director, Center for Food Safety and Applied Nutrition, Food and Drug Administration, Department of Health and Human Services, Before the Subcommittee on Health, Committee on Energy and Commerce, US House of Representatives. December 10, 2014.

2. Nathaniel Johnson, "The GM Safety Dance: What's Rule and What's Real." Grist, July 10, 2013.

3. Rachel Pomerance, "GMOs: A Breakthrough or Breakdown in US Agriculture?" *US News & World Report,* April 25, 2013.

4. Statement of Michael M. Landa, J.D., Director, Center for Food Safety and Applied Nutrition, Food and Drug Administration, Department of Health and Human Services, Before the Subcommittee on Health, Committee on Energy and Commerce, US House of Representatives. December 10, 2014.

5. William Freese and David Schubert, "Safety Testing of Genetically Engineered Food." *Biotechnology and Genetic Engineering Reviews*, November 2004, 21:299–324.

6. Correspondence from Alan M. Rulis Ph.D., Director, Office of Premarket Approval, Center for Food Safety and Applied Nutrition, US Food and Drug Administration, to Dr. Kent Croon, Regulatory Affairs Manager, Monsanto Company, September 25, 1996.

7. Joël Spiroux de Vendômois, et al., "Debate on GMOs Health Risks after Statistical Findings in Regulatory Tests." International Journal of Biological Sciences, 2010; 6(6):590–598. doi:10.7150/ijbs.6.590.

8. William Freese and David Schubert, "Safety Testing of Genetically Engineered Food." *Biotechnology and Genetic Engineering Reviews,* November 2004, 21:299–324.

9. I. M. Zdziarski, J. W. Edwards, J. A. Carman and J. I. Haynes, "GM Crops and the Rat Digestive Tract: A Critical Review." Environment International, December 2014. 73:423–433. doi: 10.1016/j.envint.2014.08.018.

10. Ben Goldacre, "Trial Sans Error: How Pharma-Funded Research Cherry-Picks Positive Results." *Scientific American,* February 13, 2013. Ben Goldacre, *Bad Pharma: How Drug Companies Mislead Doctors and Harm Patients* (New York: Faber and Faber, 2012), pp. 1–2.

11. Ben Goldacre, *Bad Pharma: How Drug Companies Mislead Doctors and Harm Patients* (New York: Faber and Faber, 2012), p. 20. See also Erick H. Turner, Annette M. Matthews, Eftihia Linardatos, Robert A. Tell, and Robert Rosenthal, "Selective Publication of Antidepressant Trials and Its Influence on Apparent Efficacy." *New England Journal of Medicine,* January 17, 2008. 2008; 358:252–260. DOI: 10.1056/NEJMsa065779. Benedict Carey, "Researchers Find a Bias Toward Upbeat Findings on Antidepressants." *New York Times,* January 17, 2008.

12. Dan Fagin, Marianne Lavelle, and the Center for Public Integrity, *Toxic Deception: How the Chemical Industry Manipulates Science, Bends the Law and Endangers Your Health* (Secaucus, NJ: Carol Publishing Group, 1996), p. 33.

13. Dan Fagin, Marianne Lavelle, and the Center for Public Integrity, *Toxic Deception: How the Chemical Industry Manipulates Science, Bends the Law and Endangers Your Health* (Secaucus, NJ: Carol Publishing Group, 1996), p. 34.

14. Joël Spiroux de Vendômois et al., "Debate on GMOs Health Risks after Statistical Findings in Regulatory Tests." International Journal of Biological Sciences, 2010; 6(6):590–598. doi:10.7150/ijbs.6.590.

15. "Food Safety: FDA and USDA Should Strengthen Pesticide Residue Monitoring Programs and Further Disclose Monitoring Limitations." US Government Accountability Office, November 6, 2014. GAO-15–38.

16. Kimberly Kindy, "Pesticide Levels on Food Unknown Due to Poor Government Testing." *Washington Post,* November 7, 2014.

17. Kurt Eichenwald, Gina Kolata, and Melody Petersen, "Biotechnology Food: From the Lab to a Debacle." *New York Times,* January 25, 2001.

18. "Statement of Policy: Foods Derived from New Plant Varieties." US Food and Drug Administration, May 29, 1992. 57 FR 22984.

19. Marian Burros, "Documents Show Officials Disagreed on Altered Food." *New York Times,* December 1, 1999.

20. Helena Paul and Ricarda Steinbrecher, *Hungry Corporations: Transnational Biotech Companies Colonise the Food Chain* (London: Zed Books, 2003), p. 170.

21. Erik Millstone, Eric Brunner, and Sue Mayer, "Beyond 'Substantial Equivalence.'" *Nature* 401, 525–526, October 7, 1999. doi:10.1038/44006.

22. "Premarket Notice Concerning Bioengineered Foods." US Food and Drug Administration, January 18, 2001. 66 FR 4706, at 4711. Memorandum from Michael Hansen, Senior Scientist, Consumer Reports, to AMA Council on Science and Public Health, "Reasons for Labeling of Genetically Engineered Foods." March 19, 2012.

> "All such studies to date have concluded, unsurprisingly, that no agriculture or food production method is risk free, whether GMO, conventional or organic, but on balance, GMOs are as safe, or safer, than other methods."

There Is Sufficient Safety Testing for GMOs

Alan McHughen

In the following viewpoint, Alan McHughen argues that proper safety review of GMOs and independent research into GM crops exists. He asserts that genetic modification is equal in safety to other agricultural or food production methods and that no case of harm has been tied to GM technology since its inception in the 1970s. McHughen is an educator, consumer advocate, and molecular geneticist with an interest in crop improvement and environmental sustainability. He helped develop US and Canadian regulations for the safety of genetically engineered crops and foods and has served as a Jefferson Science Fellow at the US Department of State.

As you read, consider the following questions:

1. According to the viewpoint, why do regulatory agencies review specific GMOs on a case-by-case basis?
2. According to the viewpoint, what three federal government agencies are responsible for assessing GMO safety in the United States?
3. According to the viewpoint, why does the data on new proposed GE varieties presented to the FDA almost never show objectionable nutritional compositions?

Calls for increased regulation do not account for the robust review already in place. The safety of GM food and crops is not in question in the scientific community. The current regulatory program ensures their safety both in the farm field and for consumers.

- Every major scientific body in the US and around the world has reviewed independent research related to GM crops and food and has concluded they are as safe as food and crops developed from other methods in use today.
- New non-genetically engineered (GE) foods and crops are continually being added to the marketplace. None of these non-GE crops undergo safety testing and review prior to commercialization even though the potential exists for changes that could be harmful, while GE crops and foods must meet rigorous standards of safety.
- GM crops and foods are regulated at every stage of production from research planning through field-testing, food and environmental safety assessment, and after commercial use.
- GM crops and foods have been in use in the US for 30 years with no evidence, despite allegations, that they cause any harm.
- GM foods contain the same nutritional attributes as like foods produced with non-GM crops (although some may contain added nutritional benefits, such as vitamin enhancements).

Any GM food with significantly lower nutritional attributes would be rejected in the regulatory process
- In decades of testing in the lab and in field trials, a transferred gene has never been known to produce a new allergen, toxin or anything functionally different from what was expected.

From Medicine to Food—Scientists Affirm the Safety of GM Technology

Since the initial development of genetic engineering more than three decades ago, there has been no scientific support for the perception among some consumers that GMOs are harmful. While no agricultural or food production method can be entirely free from risk, genetic modification (GM) is on par for safety as compared to other production methods.

Genetic engineering (GE), also called recombinant DNA (rDNA), is the underlying technology giving rise to Genetically Modified Organisms (GMOs). This process was first developed in the 1970s and used to make the first commercial GM product, human insulin, in the early 1980s. From the beginning, scientists questioned whether the GM process would result in hazardous substances. Several independent government studies in the 1980s concluded that the process of genetic engineering was not inherently hazardous (NAS, OECD).

Subsequently, additional professional scientific and medical organizations worldwide have conducted follow-up studies and reviews of existing studies as GM products have become more prevalent, not only in foods but also in medicines and industrial products, such as biofuels and detergents. All of these independent scientific analyses (British Royal Society, French Academies, etc.) support the original conclusions. Since the time that GM products were first commercialized in the 1980s, and despite allegations by some that they might pose health hazards, not a single case of harm can be attributed to GM technology. (NAS, 2004, AAAS, 2012)

In considering GMO safety, it's critical to differentiate between a specific GMO and the category consisting of all GMOs. A specific GMO could be a particular variety of corn or soybean that might conceivably produce a substance in the grain (e.g., an allergen) that could pose a health threat to a small subset of the population. In contrast, a categorical hazard—the production of a hypothetical harmful substance from all organisms undergoing the GM process—would arise from any GMO, not just certain specific ones.

We know that categorical hazards do not exist. Scientists have been studying a wide range of GMOs since the 1970s and have not identified any categorical hazards. If there is a hazard with a given GMO, it is limited to that specific GMO and not the entire spectrum of GMOs. This is why regulatory agencies review specific GMOs on a case-by-case basis. It is also why FDA and USDA decline food labels based on the process of genetic engineering, because of the process of how a food is irrelevant to food safety or nutrition.

Testing Is Extensive Prior to Commercial Release of a New GMO

When a GMO is being developed, a gene of interest (a piece of DNA carrying the genetic recipe for a specific protein imparting the desired trait) is inserted into the genome of the host species, usually in a crop such as corn or soybeans. There are several technical methods of inserting a new piece of DNA into the DNA genome, with the two most common being Agrobacterium and biolistic (aka "gene gun").

Agrobacterium tumefaciens is a common bacterium and a naturally occurring genetic engineer. In nature, the bacteria live in soil and have the ability to transfer a portion of its bacterial DNA to a plant and have it inserted into the plant's DNA, making the bacterial DNA a permanent part of the plant's genome (i.e., the total complement of DNA of that plant). The genes carried on the bacterial DNA are "read" and "expressed" by the plant cell, resulting in the production of proteins new to the plant but beneficial to the Agrobacterium. In making GM crops, scientists trick the Agrobacterium by deleting its own bacterial genes and substituting genes of interest, that is, those genes creating a desired trait in the plant. The Agrobacterium, now carrying the genes of interest, naturally transfers those useful genes to plant cells in petri dishes, and the useful genes are naturally inserted into the plant genome and become a permanent part of the plant's genetic makeup.

The other method, using the biolistic "gene gun," involves taking many copies of the gene of interest and coating them on tiny shotgun pellets, which are literally shot with a blast of air into the target plant cells in a petri dish. Again, the genes of interest are inserted into the genome of the plant cell and become a permanent part of the plant's genome.

In both cases, the engineering adds one or two additional genes to the 30,000 or so genes (depending on the species) already present in the genome. It's important to remember that the basic plant remains the same as before; genetic engineering merely adds a useful gene (or sometimes deletes a deleterious gene) to the complement of genes already present in the genome. Here's an illustrative analogy: inserting a desirable gene into a plant genome is like adding a useful app to your smartphone; the new app takes up a small bit of space and (usually) doesn't interfere with the other apps already present, but performs useful functions when called upon to do so.

Early testing of transformed (genetically engineered) cells takes place in the lab, while the recipient or host plant cells are still growing in petri dishes. Various tests are conducted to ensure that the cells have indeed taken up the transferred DNA and those successfully "transformed" cells are nurtured and grown into whole plants, which will flower and set seed, just as traditional plants of the same species. These seeds and their progeny are tested for many features, including food and environmental safety as well as the new trait of interest.

In addition to assuring that the DNA is successfully integrated into the host plant genome, tests assure that the inserted gene is actively "read" or "expressed" and that the appropriate protein is produced from the transferred gene recipe. In practice, a transferred gene either successfully produces the appropriate protein, or if unsuccessful, fails to produce anything functional.

Crucially, a transferred gene has never been known to produce a new allergen, toxin or anything functionally different from what was expected.

Years of Rigorous Testing Ensure GM Safety

Progeny testing continues into confined growth cabinets and, if all is well, then in greenhouses. At each generation, the testing becomes more elaborate. Any transgenic "event" (the regulatory term for a single genetically transformed cell grown out into a whole plant, and all subsequent generations derived from the initial transformed cell) is tested and, if failing any test, the entire event line (i.e., all the plants derived from the initial transformed cell) is culled.

Most event lines are culled due to features of the inserted gene, such as genetic instability, where the transferred gene is not permanently fixed in place in the host genome, or if the gene is not expressed sufficiently to produce enough protein to confer the desired trait. Other reasons for culling include changes from the original cultivar (a plant or group of plants selected for desirable characteristics) features, such as poor agronomic performance (especially decreased yield or delayed ripening), weak plants, or poor quality or nutritional results such as lower vitamin content than the parent variety grown under the same conditions.

By the time the transgenic plants graduate from confined indoor trials to reach open field trials, as regulated by the US Department of Agriculture, there is already a huge collection of data relating to safety, stability and expression of the new trait. In field trials, the performance is compared with other plants of the same species to ensure the agronomic performance is at least as good as the parent. Such field trials are also grown in different regions where the commercial cultivars are grown to collect data on regional performance. Other tests assure the expression of the new trait functions sufficiently under field-grown conditions, because those are the conditions under which farmers will be growing them.

These tests can take several years to complete, and only then, if all the results are satisfactory, will the GM plant be considered for regulatory approval and eventual commercialization.

Three US Regulatory Agencies Assess GMO Safety

In the US, three federal government agencies (USDA, EPA and FDA) are responsible for assuring the safety of GM crops and foods.

USDA

US Department of Agriculture (USDA) reviews prospective new genetically engineered crops to assure environmental safety, especially focusing on whether the new plants will become plant pests (a.k.a. weeds). USDA considers the species under review, asking questions about the inherent weediness of the species, the prevalence of related species that show weediness, and the ease with which the cultivated varieties might outcross (introduction of unrelated genetic material into a breeding line) with those weedy relatives. USDA also regulates the import, interstate movement and open field trials of GE plants, called in regulatory terms "Regulated Articles."

EPA

US Environmental Protection Agency (EPA) is mainly responsible for pesticides and pesticidal activities. For example, new GE crops that make new use of herbicides to control weeds or insecticides to protect against insect pests are fully investigated by EPA to assure the pesticidal use is safe and appropriate.

FDA

US Food and Drug Administration (FDA) considers food and feed safety in an effort to recognize if health hazards are present as products or substances, such as toxic chemicals (e.g., cyanide)

THE FDA's PLANT BIOTECHNOLOGY CONSULTATION PROGRAM

FDA created the Plant Biotechnology Consultation Program in the 1990s to cooperatively work with GE plant developers to help them ensure foods made from their new GE plant varieties are safe and lawful. In this program, we evaluate the safety of food from the new GE crop before it enters the market.

Although the consultation program is voluntary, GE plant developers routinely participate in it before bringing a new GE plant to market. FDA completed its first plant biotechnology consultation in 1994. Thus far, we have evaluated more than 150 GE plant varieties through this program. For a list of completed consultations, see our Biotechnology Consultations database.

During the initial consultation phase, GE plant developers meet with FDA and explain their GE product to FDA. FDA can then provide feedback about the kinds of data and information that would be important to consider in a safety assessment.

The final consultation phase begins once a GE plant developer completes its safety assessment and submits a summary of the assessment to FDA.

FDA evaluates the data and information in the summary to identify any unresolved food safety and nutritional issues or other legal considerations. Some examples of questions we ask in this evaluation include:

or biological pathogens (e.g. E. coli or Salmonella) in a food or feed consumed. In other words, methods or processes for making a given product are not inherently hazardous unless they result in a hazardous substance in the final product. Scientists at FDA focus on components of the food and feed derived from GE crops. In its investigations, FDA considers the nutrient composition of the new food and feed, looking at protein content, fiber, minerals, vitamins, amino acids and other substances in the food. FDA also focuses on allergens and toxins in the food, including pre-existing allergens and toxins as well as the possibility of introducing new allergens or toxins during the gene transfer. If any nutrient appears

- Does food from the GE plant contain a new toxin or allergen?
- Is food from the GE plant as nutritious as that from its traditionally bred counterpart?

If FDA identifies an issue that needs to be addressed, we work with the developers to get the information needed to resolve it.

When all safety and other regulatory issues are resolved, and the data and information logically support the conclusion that food from the new plant variety will be as safe as food from conventionally bred varieties, we conclude the consultation with a letter to the GE plant developer. The letter reminds the developer that they remain legally obligated to ensure the safety of the food products they bring to market.

Finally, FDA posts the relevant information and documentation to the Biotechnology Consultations on Food from GE Plant Varieties section of its website for public viewing. The posting includes the following items:

- Submission date
- Developer name and contact information
- Basic information about the GE plant variety
- The FDA response letter
- A memo summarizing the data and information FDA evaluated

"How FDA Regulates Food from Genetically Engineered Plants," US Food and Drug Administration, January 4, 2018.

to be significantly higher or lower than what is seen in that species, the GE line is rejected.

In practice, the company or other developer collects such information for years prior to going to FDA, so they will already have culled any such variant lines. By the time FDA scientists see the proposed new GE variety, the data will almost invariably show no differences in nutritional composition, apart from the intended changes associated with the introduced trait. All GE crops and foods on the market have passed this FDA review.

New crops and foods are constantly being added to the marketplace, developed using an array of methods, including traditional crossing, ionizing radiation mutagenesis, organics and simple introductions from overseas. None of these non-GE crops undergo safety testing and review prior to commercialization even though the potential exists for changes that could be harmful, while GE crops and foods must meet rigorous standards of safety.

Assessing the Safety of GMOs—The Scientific Community Consensus

In addition to US government agencies assessing the safety of GMOs, various professional, scientific, and medical bodies worldwide have also investigated the safety of GMOs. Those independent professional bodies usually appoint a blue-ribbon panel of a dozen or so experts in the relevant fields, including genetics, medicine, nutrition, agronomy, etc., and spend as long as two years on the investigation. A final report from the panel issues the findings.

All such studies to date have concluded, unsurprisingly, that no agriculture or food production method is risk free, whether GMO, conventional or organic, but on balance, GMOs are as safe, or safer, than other methods.

The Genetic Literacy Project notes that over 2,000 global studies affirm the food and environmental safety of GM. Below is a list of some of the leading scientific bodies that have affirmed the safety of GM foods and crops:

- US National Academies
- US Institute of Medicine
- American Medical Association
- British Royal Society
- Royal Society of Medicine
- European Food Safety Authority
- EU Economic Commission
- World Health Organization
- American Association for the Advancement of Science
- American Dietetic Association
- International Seed Foundation

Periodical and Internet Sources Bibliography

The following articles have been selected to supplement the diverse views presented in this chapter.

John Conyers, "Let Americans Know What's in Their Food," *CNN,* July 22, 2015. https://www.cnn.com/2015/07/22/opinions/ conyers-gmo-label-bill/index.html

Frederick Rowe Davis, "The Real Scandal at the EPA? It's Not Keeping Us Safe," *The Washington Post,* February 26, 2018. https://www.washingtonpost.com/news/made-by-history/ wp/2018/02/26/the-real-scandal-at-the-epa-its-not-keeping-us- safe/?noredirect=on&utm_term=.ffeacb5fb3d7

Maggie Fox, "There's No Need to Label GMO Plants, FDA Says," *NBC News,* November 23, 2015. https://www.nbcnews.com/health/ health-news/theres-no-need-label-gmo-plants-fda-says-n468301

Carey Gillam, "US Review of GMO Crops Finds Risks and Rewards, Says More Transparency Needed," *The Huffington Post,* May 17, 2016. https://www.huffingtonpost.com/carey-gillam/us-review- of-gmo-crops-fi_b_10006254.html

Amy Harmon, "How Square Watermelons Get Their Shape, and Other G.M.O. Misconceptions," *New York Times,* August 2, 2016. https://www.nytimes.com/interactive/2016/07/12/science/gmo- misconceptions.html

Paul Koberstein, "EPA Mulls Ban on Nation's Most Heavily Used Insecticide," *Salon,* January 30, 2016. https://www.salon. com/2016/01/30/why_the_potential_epa_ban_on_the_nations_ most_heavily_used_insecticide_pins_farmers_between_a_rock_ and_a_hard_place_partner/

Freya Wilson, "Commercial Pesticides: Not As Safe As They Seem," Frontiers, March 15, 2018. https://blog.frontiersin. org/2018/03/15/public-health-commercial-pesticide-adjuvant- risks/

For Further Discussion

Chapter 1

1. Nick Mole proposes a fundamental shift into utilizing pesticides as a last resort instead of as a first measure. Do you think this is a reasonable course of action? Why, or why not?
2. Do you agree that it's important to factor in externalities when calculating the cost of pesticides? Explain your reasoning.
3. The Insecticide Resistance Action Committee recommends several resistance management strategies including IPM-based programs, protecting beneficial arthropods when applying insecticides, and destroying crop residue to deprive insects of food and winter shelters. Do these practices seem feasible for most growers? Why, or why not?

Chapter 2

1. Miguel Altieri and Clara Nicholls argue that modern agriculture practices have had severe negative impacts on the environment. Does the evidence they provide seem strong enough to support their argument? Why, or why not?
2. To determine who has benefited the most from GMOs, Nathanael Johnson consults various experts in the industry. Which statement do you agree with? Explain your reasoning.
3. Sarah Armstrong and John Clough claim that pesticide use is a necessary part of the solution to global food shortages, while Felicity Lawrence asserts that this model of farming is counterproductive to the goal of food security. Which argument do you find more persuasive? Explain your reasoning.

Chapter 3

1. Mark Lynas declares that there is nothing left to debate on whether GMOs are safe, but Angelika Hilbeck et al. contend that there are many issues with the claim of a scientific consensus existing on GMO safety. Do you agree with Hilbeck et al.? Why, or why not?
2. Kelly Servick notes that public skepticism of GE crops continues despite recurring reports on their safety. Do you find the reports' findings to be convincing or is the evidence lacking? Explain your reasoning.
3. The American Society of Plant Biologists points out that when we're introduced to new foods in our diet from exotic crops, we rarely ask the questions we ask about GM crops. Why do you think this discrepancy in behavior exists?

Chapter 4

1. Frank Eyhorn states that while most industry-financed research studies find few health risks to pesticides if used properly, hundreds of scientific studies in renowned journals have found serious health hazards. How would you explain this discrepancy in findings? Do you think there is a reasonable explanation? Why, or why not?
2. Mark Fergusson pushes for the implementation of GMO labeling, asserting the need for transparency to consumers. On the other hand, Steve Armstrong raises concerns about the challenges of transparency and cautions that labeling can mislead consumers instead. Which argument do you find more persuasive? Explain your reasoning.
3. Alan McHughen argues that sufficient safety testing and regulations already exist for GMOs. What evidence does he give to support his argument? Do you agree with his claim? Why, or why not?

Organizations to Contact

The editors have compiled the following list of organizations concerned with the issues debated in this book. The descriptions are derived from materials provided by the organizations. All have publications or information available for interested readers. The list was compiled on the date of publication of the present volume; the information provided here may change. Be aware that many organizations take several weeks or longer to respond to inquiries, so allow as much time as possible.

Beyond Pesticides

701 E Street, SE, Suite 200, Washington, DC 20003
(202) 543-5450
email: info@beyondpesticides.org
website: www.beyondpesticides.org

Beyond Pesticides is a nonprofit organization that educates the public on pesticides and alternative options, equipping people with the knowledge to protect themselves and the environment.

Center for Food Safety

660 Pennsylvania Avenue, SE, #402, Washington, DC 20003
(202) 547-9359
email: office@centerforfoodsafety.org
website: www.centerforfoodsafety.org

Center for Food Safety (CFS) is a national non-profit and environmental advocacy organization that works to protect human health and the environment. CFS seeks to reduce the use of harmful food production methods and instead promote organic and other forms of sustainable agriculture.

Center for Health, Environment & Justice

7139 Shreve Road, Falls Church, VA 22046
(703) 237-2249
email: info@chej.org
website: www.chej.org

The Center for Health, Environment & Justice (CHEJ) is a leading national resource for grassroots environmental activism. CHEJ has built a broad network of environmental advocates and unites community voices from nationwide on diverse environmental health issues.

Environmental Protection Agency (EPA)

1200 Pennsylvania Avenue, NW, Washington, DC 20460
(202) 564-4700
website: www.epa.gov

The EPA's mission is to protect human health and the environment, and it achieves this goal by developing and enforcing regulations, giving grants, studying environmental issues, sponsoring partnerships, and informing the public about the environment.

Genetic Literacy Project

1120 Welsh Road, Suite 200, North Wales, PA 19454
(410) 941-9374
email: info@geneticliteracyproject.org
website: www.geneticliteracyproject.org

The goal of the Genetic Literacy Project (GLP) is to aid the public in separating science from legislation, facilitate cooperation between researchers, and encourage the breakthrough development of ethically and scientifically sound genetic technologies.

IPM Institute of North America

211 S. Paterson Street, Suite 380, Madison, WI 53703
(608) 232-1410
email: info@ipminstitute.org
website: www.ipminstitute.org

The IPM Institute of North America is an independent non-profit for the improvement of sustainability in agriculture and communities through practices like the market-based mechanisms in Integrated Pest Management (IPM).

Non-GMO Project

1155 N. State Street, Suite #502, Bellingham, WA 98225
(360) 255-7704
email: info@nongmoproject.org
website: www.nongmoproject.org

The Non-GMO Project is a non-profit organization dedicated to preserving and building sources of non-GMO products, educating consumers, and providing product choices that are verified to be non-GMO.

Pan American Health Organization

525 23rd Street, NW, Washington, DC 20037
(202) 974-3000
website: www.paho.org

The Pan American Health Organization (PAHO) is the specialized health agency of the Americas and the Regional Office of the Americas for the World Health Organization (WHO), the specialized health agency of the United Nations. PAHO's mission is to promote equity in health, combat disease, and improve the quality of life of the people in the Americas.

Pesticide Action Network North America

2029 University Avenue, Suite 200, Berkeley, CA 94704
(510) 788-9020
website: www.panna.org

Pesticide Action Network (PAN) North America seeks to create a healthy and thriving food system by replacing hazardous pesticides with ecologically sound and socially just alternatives.

Bibliography of Books

Mike Adams. *Food Forensics: the Hidden Toxins Lurking in Your Food and How You Can Avoid Them for Lifelong Health.* Dallas, TX: BenBella Books, 2016.

Rachel Carson. *Silent Spring.* Boston, MA: Houghton Mifflin Harcourt, 1962.

Jennifer Clapp. *Hunger in the Balance: The New Politics of International Food Aid.* Ithaca, NY: Cornell University Press, 2012.

Steven Druker. *Altered Genes, Twisted Truth: How the Venture to Genetically Engineer Our Food Has Subverted Science, Corrupted Government, and Systematically Deceived the Public.* Fairfield, IA: Clear River Press, 2015.

Renee Dufault. *Unsafe at Any Meal.* Garden City Park, NY: Square One Publishers, 2017.

Charles Duncan. *Eat, Drink, and Be Wary: How Unsafe Is Our Food?* Lanham, MD: Rowman & Littlefield, 2015.

Carey Gillam. *Whitewash: The Story of a Weed Killer, Cancer, and the Corruption of Science.* Washington, DC: Island Press, 2017.

McKay Jenkins. *ContamiNation: My Quest to Survive in a Toxic World.* New York, NY: Avery, 2016.

Sheldon Krimsky and Jeremy Gruber. *The GMO Deception: What You Need to Know about Food, Corporations, and Government Agencies Putting Our Families and Our Environment at Risk.* New York, NY: Skyhorse Publishing, 2016.

Bill Lambrecht. *Dinner at the New Gene Café: How Genetic Engineering Is Changing What We Eat, How We Live, and the Global Politics of Food.* New York, NY: St. Martins Press, 2001.

André Leu. *The Myths of Safe Pesticides.* Greely, CO: Acres U.S.A., 2014.

Mark Lynas. *Seeds of Science: Why We Got It So Wrong on GMOs.* New York, NY: Bloomsbury Sigma, 2018.

Michelle Mart. *Pesticides, a Love Story: America's Enduring Embrace of Dangerous Chemicals.* Lawrence, KS: University Press of Kansas, 2015.

Emily Monosson. *Unnatural Selection: How We Are Changing Life, Gene by Gene.* Washington, DC: Island Press, 2015.

Robert Paarlberg. *Food Politics: What Everyone Needs to Know.* New York, NY: Oxford University Press, 2013.

Marie-Monique Robin. *Our Daily Poison: From Pesticides to Packaging, How Chemicals Have Contaminated the Food Chain and Are Making Us Sick.* New York, NY: The New Press, 2014.

Marie-Monique Robin. *The World According to Monsanto.* New York, NY: The New Press, 2012.

Claire Robinson, Michael Antoniou, and John Fagan. *GMO Myths and Truths: A Citizen's Guide to the Evidence on the Safety and Efficacy of Genetically Modified Crops and Foods.* White River Junction, VT: Chelsea Green Publishing, 2015.

E. G. Vallianatos and McKay Jenkins. *Poison Spring: The Secret History of Pollution and the EPA.* New York, NY: Bloomsbury Press, 2014.

Index